doctrine & covenants

big picture/little picture
STUDY GUIDE

by Cali Black
creator of @comefollowmestudy

what to expect

Hey! I am SO glad that you are here.

I love the scriptures, and I love feeling confident while I read. When I used to try to "study the scriptures", I would often feel confused, and I didn't really have a great experience. I felt like everyone else "got it", and I was stuck with a kid-level understanding.

I've spent years trying to learn about the background info for all of these intricate scripture stories. I've learned about people, symbolism, cultural differences, and facts galore.

But I also know that most people don't have time to read elaborate and detailed historical books in order to learn all of this for yourselves.

So I started creating study guides that were for people like me. Latter-day Saints who:
- **want to feel like they understand the scriptures more**
- **but don't have much extra time to devote to figuring it out**

As a former middle school teacher, I like to think I've mastered the art of simplification. I've taken countless hours of research and distilled them into what you REALLY need to know.

And then I realized that even more important than actually understanding what's going on in the scriptures, is figuring out how to <u>apply</u> them to my life and have them help to change me each day that I open their pages.

And thus, my Big Picture/Little Picture Study Guides were born.

The perfect mix of content, short summaries, connections, and a whole bunch of spiritual focus. I think it's a pretty good recipe.

If you've never used a Big Picture/Little Picture Study Guide, here's what to expect:

Each week, I give you EVERYTHING that you need to be successful on both ends of the scripture study spectrum: the background knowledge AND the spiritual application.

BIG PICTURE

In the Big Picture section, I give you whatever historical, contextual, or interesting knowledge I think that you'll need to totally "get" what's going on. (In simple, bullet-point form, of course.)

LITTLE PICTURE

After all that big context, we get to the nitty-gritty daily reading part.

I give a quick little reference for every single section that we read, including a couple of sentences about what you should know/remember BEFORE you read, and then a simple summary of WHAT you are reading in that section. (Just in case things get confusing!)

And since there is so much historical info in the Doctrine and Covenants, I also give you quick references for who each revelation was through, to, and where and when it was received.

SPIRITUAL GUIDING QUESTIONS

This is, of course, where the rubber meets the road in WHY we study the scriptures. I've created 7 questions for you to ponder each week, so you could respond to one each day, do them all at once, or pick and choose which questions resonate with you. Hint: These also work as great questions to ask if you are teaching a class this Sunday!

Pretty much, I've packed as much info into this little study guide as I could while still keeping a conversational feel, because talking about the scriptures is super fun.

If you've been wanting to feel "in the know" before Sunday School lessons, if you've been looking for an easier way to understand the scriptures in order to teach your kids, if you've been looking to boost your knowledge before YOU stand up and teach seminary, then I believe this study guide is exactly what you need.

Above all though, never let this study guide, or anything else for that matter, separate you from getting in the actual scriptures. In fact, I hope this guide encourages you to get in the scriptures more often. Nothing is more important than you, with the Spirit, reading the word of God!

I am so excited to help orient you in the Doctrine and Covenants this year. This first quarter is a whirlwind of people, places, and events that you've probably heard of before, but maybe don't fully remember. That's why I've kept it simple - because beneath all the craziness, there are some powerful examples of faith, revelation, and learning to trust God.

For ease, this study guide has been broken into quarters for the year. Be sure to look for the remaining April–June, July–September, and October–December study guides as those months roll around on comefollowmestudy.com or on Amazon.

I love connecting with people and talking about the scriptures, so make sure you follow me on Instagram @comefollowmestudy, on Facebook.com/comefollowmestudy, or join my email list at comefollowmestudy.com. I also co-host the One Minute Scripture Study podcast wherever you listen to podcasts!

Alright, are you feeling ready?! Let's go! Happy Studying!

- Cali Black

cool features

For each week this quarter, you'll find:

General Context: These bullet points remind your brain what we studied the week before, and give you any context you need for the current reading in order to connect the story together.

Spiritual Themes: Sometimes there is so much stuff in a reading assignment that it's hard to know where to focus! That's why you'll get three spiritual themes each week to help you focus on some of the most important topics. These would be great to highlight or note in your scriptures as you actually study, or you can just keep them in mind to guide you as you read through the assigned readings. If you are a gospel teacher, these can also help to serve as lesson outlines.

People to Know: This is a quick bullet point list that includes descriptions and extra info about people. Anyone that is mentioned in that week's reading, or is an important part of the historical context or backstory, gets put on the list so that you always have an easy reference, especially if you need to jog your memory on who they are.

Places to Know: This bullet point list gives a quick rundown of all the locations mentioned in that week's reading. Having a good grasp on where stories are taking place, and who is from where, can make a huge difference in understanding these scriptures.

Section Breakdowns: Often, we aren't sitting down to read the entire week's reading in one sitting. So if you read all the general context, feel like you totally "get it", and then read one section. . . When you sit down to read the next day, it may have all disappeared from your brain. That's why I give you a "BEFORE YOU READ" quick reminder before every single section. I also give a "WHAT YOU'LL READ" with a section summary in case you want to double check you understood what you just read. You'll also get easy references for who each revelation was given to and through, as well as where and when it was received.

Spiritual Guiding Questions: This is where you get to put your own pencil to the paper and practice applying the scriptures. There are seven questions for each week, so you could ponder one each day, do them all at one time, or only focus on the questions that resonate with you. These also make great discussion questions if you are a teacher!

historical maps

A spiritual Restoration that started in a single sacred grove soon involved many important locations in 1800's America!

It always helps my brain to be able to keep track of locations if I can actually see them on a map.

So each week, I've included a simple map made by the amazing Sarah Cook from Olivet Designs. She went through each section and created an easy-to-read, clear map that highlights the locations where important events happened.

You are going to LOVE referencing these maps each week, especially when you want to better understand the distance between important locations in early church history. Plus, the maps are super cute.

In addition to weekly historical maps specific to each reading, Sarah also created a master map with ALL the essential locations mentioned throughout the Doctrine & Covenants.

It's something you'll want to come back to that will help you understand how these locations fit into the continental United States in the 1800's, and will add some BIG PICTURE understanding as we learn about the growth and movement of the young church this year.

Again, a huge thank you to Sarah Cook from Olivet Designs for allowing me to share these super useful maps with you this year.

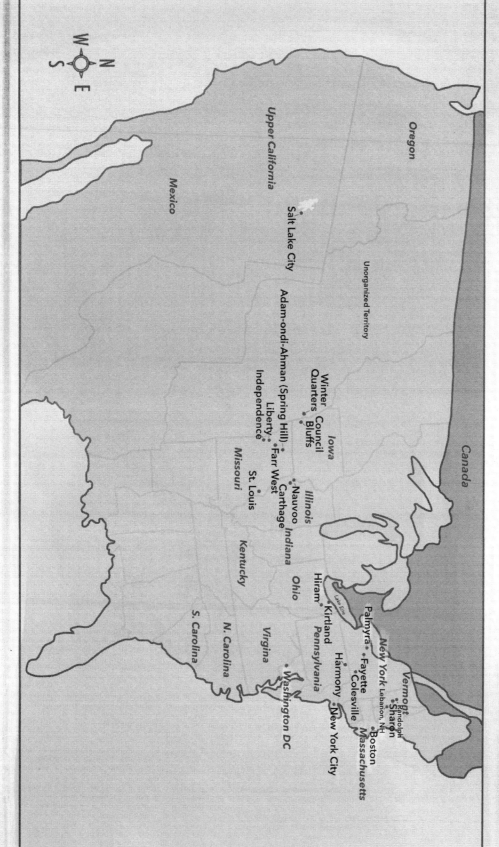

United States of America

in the early 1800s

THE RESTORATION PROCLAMATION

"The Promised Restoration Goes Forward"

BIG PICTURE

How to feel confident fitting in this week's readings with the entire Doctrine & Covenants

General Context:

- **This year's study of the Doctrine and Covenants starts with an event that you probably were alive to witness!** While that may seem a little strange, there is power in recognizing that while the Restoration of the gospel of Jesus Christ is something that may have started a couple hundred years ago, this process most certainly continues today.

- **On April 5, 2020, President Russell M. Nelson read a document during his talk in General Conference** titled, "The Restoration of the Fullness of the Gospel of Jesus Christ: A Bicentennial Proclamation to the World" (commonly referred to as the "Restoration Proclamation"). The word "bicentennial" means 200 years, and while we do not know the exact date of Joseph Smith's First Vision, Joseph mentions that it occurred on a spring morning in 1820. President Nelson, the other members of the First Presidency, and the members of the Quorum of the Twelve apostles wanted to celebrate 200 years since the beginning of the Restoration of the gospel of Jesus Christ by creating a document that would proclaim to the entire world the reality of Joseph Smith's vision, the role that Joseph Smith played in the Restoration of various gospel elements (including the Book of Mormon and priesthood power), and the impact that this Restoration continues to have on Saints around the globe today.

- **If you remember the spring of 2020, you might remember that General Conference was very different that particular April.** As the world grappled with the beginning of the COVID-19 pandemic, the Church announced that General Conference would occur without an audience. It was held in the Church Office Building, with pre-recorded music and only those speaking or praying in attendance. In the Sunday morning session on April 5, 2020, President Nelson began his talk, titled "Hear Him". During this talk, the actual Restoration Proclamation was introduced through a recording of President Nelson reading the words of the Proclamation in the Sacred Grove in Palmyra, New York. After the video recording played, President Russell M. Nelson also led the Church in a worldwide solemn assembly and Hosanna Shout, accompanied by the singing of "The Spirit of God".

Spiritual Themes:

Look for these themes as you read this week! Find examples in the scriptures, and ponder on what these themes can look like in your life.

- **Personal Revelation is Available to Those Who "Hear Him"**

- **God Uses Prophets to Further His Work**

- **The Restoration is Ongoing**

People to Know:

- **The Authors of the Restoration Proclamation**
  - **Members of the First Presidency:** Russell M. Nelson, Dallin H. Oaks, Henry B. Eyring
  - **Members of the Quorum of the Twelve Apostles:** M. Russell Ballard, Jeffrey R. Holland, Dieter F. Uchtdorf, David A. Bednar, Quentin L. Cook, D. Todd Christofferson, Neil L. Andersen, Ronald A. Rasband, Gary E. Stevenson, Dale G. Renlund, Gerrit W. Gong, Ulisses Soares
- **People Mentioned in the Proclamation:**
  - **Joseph Smith:** The first prophet of this dispensation. He witnessed the First Vision, translated the Book of Mormon, received the priesthood, organized the Church, and was ultimately martyred in 1844.
  - **John the Baptist:** Jesus Christ's cousin who prepared the way for the Savior and baptized Him. He appeared in his resurrected form to Joseph Smith and Oliver Cowdery on May 15, 1829 and restored the Aaronic priesthood.
  - **Peter, James, and John:** Jesus Christ's original apostles in the New Testament church. They appeared to Joseph Smith and Oliver Cowdery and restored the Melchizedek priesthood.
  - **Elijah:** A prophet from Old Testament times who helped Israel turn away from false prophets. He appeared to Joseph Smith and Oliver Cowdery in the Kirtland, Ohio temple in 1836, restoring the sealing power.

Where are We?

- **Church Office Building, Salt Lake City, Utah**
  - On April 5, 2020, President Nelson shared the Proclamation Restoration as part of his General Conference address.
- **Sacred Grove, Palmyra, New York**
  - In the spring of 1820, Joseph Smith saw a vision of God the Father and Jesus Christ, and the Restoration of the fullness of the gospel of Jesus Christ began.

LITTLE PICTURE

How to understand each section and apply principles to my life

- **The Restoration of the Fulness of the Gospel of Jesus Christ: A Bicentennial Proclamation to the World**

  - **Before You Read:** This proclamation was read to the Church by President Russell M. Nelson during the April 2020 General Conference, which marked the 200th anniversary of Joseph Smith's First Vision. It is meant as a testimony to the world from prophets and apostles of the Restoration of the gospel.

  - **What You'll Read About:** The First Presidency and Quorum of the Twelve Apostles testify of God's love, and the sacrifice of our Savior. 200 years ago, Joseph Smith saw a vision that would usher in the Restoration of God's true Church. God restored His Church through Joseph Smith with the help of heavenly visitors, and brought forth the Book of Mormon. The Church is built on the cornerstone of our Savior Jesus Christ, and millions have since embraced its truth.

SPIRITUAL GUIDING QUESTIONS

Question: This proclamation is all about the Restoration, but what is the first paragraph all about? Why do you think that's significant?

Question: Why is it important to have a testimony of Joseph Smith and the First Vision?

Question: What are some specific ways that priesthood authority has blessed and changed your life? Think about the Aaronic priesthood, the Melchizedek priesthood, and the sealing power.

Question: How has the Book of Mormon brought you closer to Jesus Christ? How can your testimony of the Book of Mormon bolster your testimony of Joseph Smith as a prophet of God?

Question: How can you better try to make Jesus Christ the chief cornerstone of your life?

Question: What are some elements of the Restoration of the gospel you've been able to witness in your lifetime? How can you keep your heart prepared to receive even more knowledge and change in the future?

Question: What promise do the apostles give in the last paragraph of the proclamation? How can you take their promise and invitation seriously this week?

ADDITIONAL THOUGHTS AND NOTES

D&C 1

"Hearken, O Ye People"

BIG PICTURE

How to feel confident fitting in this week's readings with the entire Doctrine & Covenants

General Context:

- **The very first section in the Doctrine and Covenants takes us to. . . NOT the start of the Restoration story.** (Don't worry, next week we will finally dive into the beginning!)

- **The good news is that you do not need to already know everything about Church history to get the gist of why we have this section first.** While most revelations in the Doctrine and Covenants are given to specific people in specific places for specific reasons, the Lord gave Joseph Smith the words in this section in order to serve as a "preface" for the entire world before they start to read the Doctrine and Covenants. The Lord wants us to read D&C 1 in order to understand what themes, priorities, and purposes He will display as we read the revelations contained in this book. It is the perfect place for us to begin our studies!

- **The actual context for why Joseph Smith even asked the Lord for a preface for the Doctrine and Covenants is interesting.** Picture a young but strong Church, about a year and a half old. Church members were mostly living in Ohio, scattered around the Kirtland and Hiram areas. A man named Ezra Booth had joined the Church, gotten to know Joseph Smith, and then started to become disaffected after some disagreements with the prophet. Ezra Booth ended up publishing a letter in the local newspaper with criticisms about Joseph, including accusations that Joseph was secretly receiving revelations and false prophecies. These criticisms caused Joseph to call a meeting of the elders of the Church to discuss the possibility of actually publishing all of the revelations he had received so far, which would take away their secrecy and negate Ezra Booth's arguments. At the meeting, the elders debated whether or not this would be a good idea to release all of the revelations. Many argued that this would open the Church up to even more criticism, and others were concerned about displaying the weakness of Joseph's writings. However, everyone ultimately came to an agreement that it was God's will to publish the revelations in a compilation called "The Book of Commandments". Although a group of skilled men were tasked with writing a good preface that would sufficiently introduce readers to the revelations, when they presented it at the conference, their preface was rejected by the elders. Joseph Smith then prayed to the Lord, and started to dictate the words that became the preface to the Book of Commandments, which are the same words now found in Section 1 of the Doctrine and Covenants.

Spiritual Themes:

Look for these themes as you read this week! Find examples in the scriptures, and ponder on what these themes can look like in your life.

- **The Lord's Doctrine and the Lord's Covenants**

- **Apostasy and Restoration**

- **The Role of God's Servants**

People to Know:

- **Ezra Booth**
  - Although no names are mentioned in this section, Ezra Booth's criticisms of Joseph Smith inspired the conference of elders and the subsequent publishing of the Book of Commandments. Ezra originally joined the church after seeing Joseph heal a paralyzed woman's arm. He later traveled with the prophet and Isaac Morley from Kirtland to Missouri for the first look at where Zion would be built. Ezra was not impressed, and quarreled with Joseph on the way back to Kirtland. The Lord mentioned that Ezra had not kept the laws or commandments during a revelation in September 1831 (Section 64), and Ezra published a letter in the local newspaper accusing Joseph of hiding secret plans from the public and making false prophecies. This actually ended up prompting Joseph to publish his revelations thus far in the "Book of Commandments", the precursor to the Doctrine and Covenants.

Where are We?

- **Hiram, Ohio**
  - Hiram was near Kirtland, Ohio, and this is where the John Johnson home was. The Johnson family welcomed Joseph and Emma into their home during the summer of 1831. Joseph made great progress on his translation of the Bible here. In November 1831, after Ezra Booth had started publishing terrible letters in the local newspaper about Joseph's secrecy, Joseph called a meeting of the church elders and proposed they publish all of his revelations so far in a Book of Commandments. This proposal was ratified, and the Lord gave them a revelation to use as the preface to the book (now D&C 1).

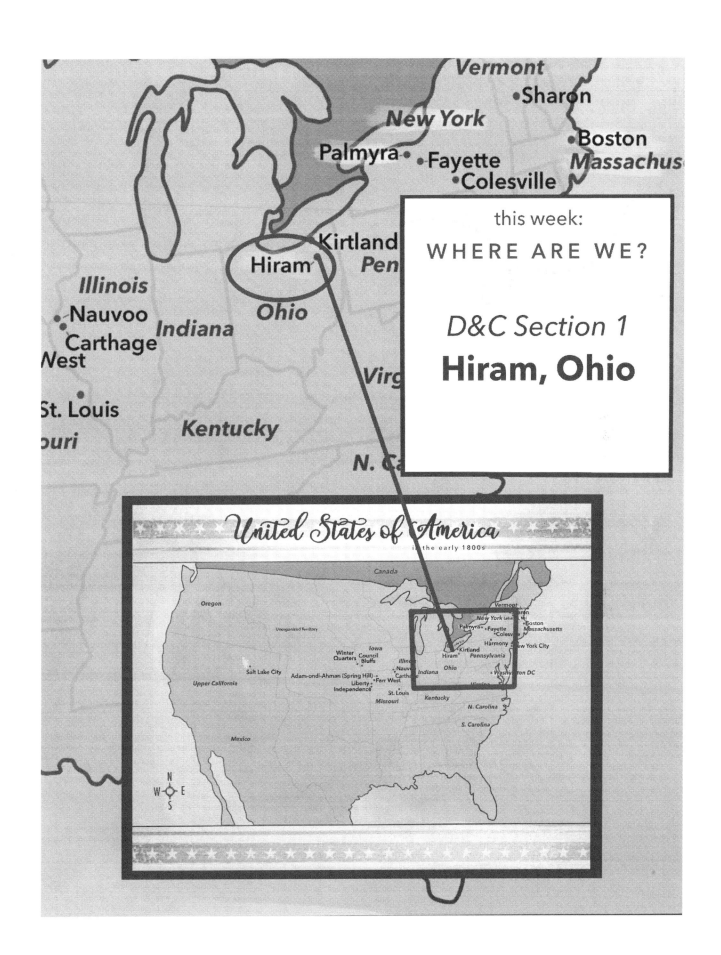

Vermont
•Sharon
New York
•Boston
Massachus
Palmyra• •Fayette
•Colesville

Kirtland
Hiram Pen
Illinois
Ohio
Nauvoo Indiana
Carthage
West
Virg
St. Louis
ouri
Kentucky
N. Ca

this week:

WHERE ARE WE?

D&C Section 1
Hiram, Ohio

United States of America
in the early 1800s

LITTLE PICTURE

How to understand each section and apply principles to my life

- **D&C 1:**
    - **Revelation Given Through:** Joseph Smith
    - **Revelation Given To:** the entire Church
    - **Revelation Given When/Where:** November 1831 in Hiram, Ohio
    - **Before You Read:** Even though most sections are chronological, the revelation for D&C 1 was actually given after D&C 66 at a special church conference. At this conference, the elders of the church agreed that all of these revelations (called the Book of Commandments at the time), should be compiled and published. The Lord gave this revelation as the "preface" to the Book of Commandments, which is why it is labeled as the first section.
    - **What You'll Read About:** The Lord tells us to hearken to the word of the Lord and the prophets, and He declares the Church to be true. God works through the weak and simple to show His power, and He invites all to repent and be forgiven. We are asked to prepare the way of the Lord and to study the commandments and doctrine found in this book.

SPIRITUAL GUIDING QUESTIONS

Question: What does it mean to "hearken" to the Lord and to His prophets? What is an example you can think of where you have hearkened? (D&C 1:1)

Question: According to these verses, why are these commandments given? (D&C 1:19-23)

Question: What do you think it means that God gives commandments "after the manner of [our] language"? Why would this be a priority to God? (D&C 1:24)

Question: What is God's stance on sin, repentance, and forgiveness? What is something you can work on repenting from right now? (D&C 1:30-33)

Question: Why does the Lord want us to search the prophecies contained in this book? Why do you personally want to study these revelations? (D&C 1:37)

Question: What themes or topics did you notice in this section that you can look for as you study all of the revelations in the Doctrine and Covenants? (D&C 1)

Question: Considering that the original name for this collection was "The Book of Commandments" and that it is now called "The Doctrine and Covenants", what do you notice the Lord teaches about commandments, doctrine, and covenants in this section? (D&C 1)

ADDITIONAL THOUGHTS AND NOTES

JOSEPH SMITH-HISTORY 1:1-26

"I Saw a Pillar of Light"

BIG PICTURE

How to feel confident fitting in this week's readings with the entire Doctrine & Covenants

General Context:

- **It is now time to start at the very beginning of the story of the Restoration!** The first section of Joseph Smith-History that we will study this week covers what we refer to as the "First Vision".

- **You'll notice at the top of Joseph Smith-History that the subheading says "Extracts From the History of Joseph Smith, the Prophet".** The 75 verses included in our scriptures are just a portion of a life history that Joseph Smith wrote in 1838. We'll study the section of his life history on the First Vision this week, we'll study the part about the coming forth of the Book of Mormon next week, and in a couple weeks we will read the final verses about the Restoration of the priesthood.

- **Where does Joseph Smith-History come from in the first place?** Joseph wrote this personal history in 1838, which was a very tumultuous time for him as Church members were transitioning from Ohio to Missouri. Joseph was also facing mounds of criticism and accusations from those outside of the Church, mostly originating with those who were afraid of the Church's political power. It was at this time that Joseph first attempted to write an official record of his experiences with the Restoration of the gospel, which had first begun 18 years prior. He had written two other records of the First Vision in personal journals prior to this, but his 1838 record was one that he knew was going to be published and was the first record that attempted to walk the public through what happened throughout various stages of the Restoration and the origin of the Church. After writing the account, Joseph's history was first published in 1842 in the Church's newspaper *Times and Seasons* in Nauvoo, Illinois. When the Church wanted to create pamphlets for missionaries to take on their trips, a portion of Joseph's history was published in the pamphlets. This portion that went out with missionaries ultimately became part of the Pearl of Great Price. That is how this portion, consisting of 75 verses, of Joseph Smith's written history became canonized in our scripture as "Joseph Smith-History".

- **And what about the context for the First Vision itself?** Joseph Smith actually does a great job in his history at setting the scene for what was going on prior to his First Vision experience at age 14. Try to immerse yourself in the world that he describes in the first few verses! Moving forward, we will be following Church history in chronological order, so settle in and welcome to 1820.

Spiritual Themes:

Look for these themes as you read this week! Find examples in the scriptures, and ponder on what these themes can look like in your life.

- **Receiving Answers to Prayers**

- **Finding Guidance in the Scriptures**

- **Opposition Comes against Good Things**

People to Know:

- **Joseph Smith Jr.**
  - The prophet of the Restoration, he originally saw God the Father and Jesus Christ in 1820.
- **Joseph Smith Sr.**
  - The father to Joseph Smith Jr. He was very supportive of his son and was the first person that young Joseph told about many of his visions. He was eventually one of the Eight Witnesses of the Book of Mormon.
- **Lucy Mack Smith**
  - The mother to Joseph Smith Jr. She was very religious and taught her children how to read the Bible. She was eagerly baptized soon after the Church was organized.
- **Joseph Smith Jr.'s siblings:**
  - Alvin, Hyrum, Samuel Harrison, William, Don Carlos, Sophronia, Catherine, and Lucy
  - Hyrum and Samuel are both named in other Doctrine and Covenants sections, as they were both included in the Eight Witnesses of the Book of Mormon and served missions in the early Church.

Where are We?

- **Manchester, New York**
  - In the spring of 1820, this was where the Smith family farm was located.

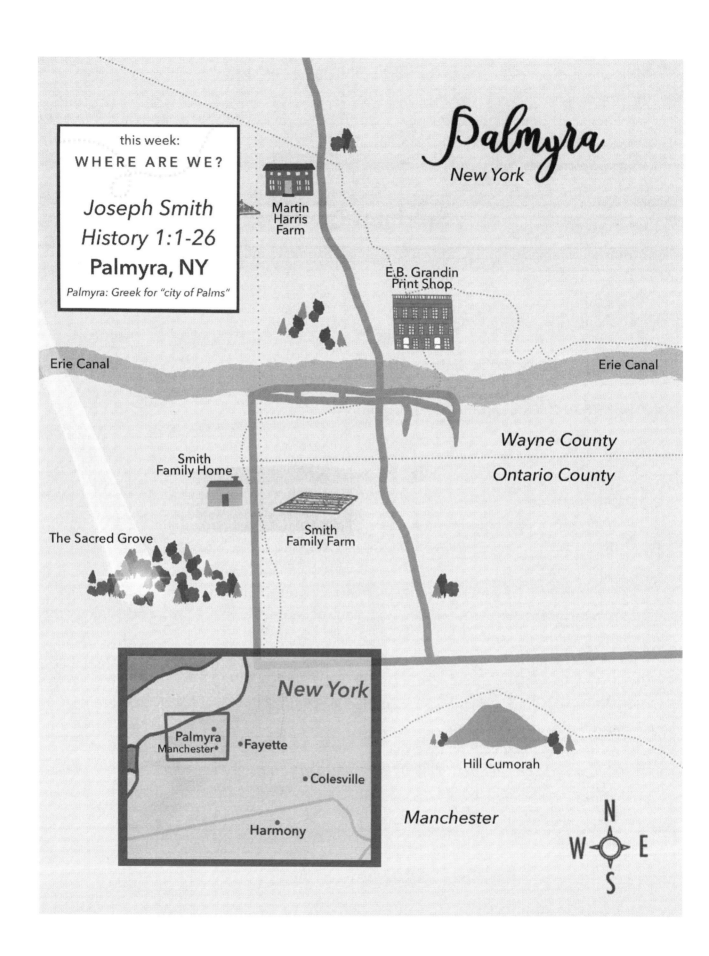

this week:

WHERE ARE WE?

Joseph Smith History 1:1-26
Palmyra, NY

Palmyra: Greek for "city of Palms"

Palmyra
New York

Martin Harris Farm

E.B. Grandin Print Shop

Erie Canal

Erie Canal

Wayne County

Ontario County

Smith Family Home

The Sacred Grove

Smith Family Farm

New York

Palmyra
Manchester• •Fayette

• Colesville

Harmony

Hill Cumorah

Manchester

N
W — E
S

LITTLE PICTURE

How to understand each section and apply principles to my life

- **Joseph Smith-History 1:1-26**

  - **Before You Read:** Joseph Smith recorded this account in 1838, 18 years after the original First Vision, as a way for him to communicate an official account of his life leading up to the organization of the Church. The verses in this section focus on the experience now known as the First Vision in 1820.

  - **What You'll Read About:** Joseph Smith describes his family and their circumstances in his early life. He tells about a religious excitement in his area, and that he was confused and concerned for the welfare of his soul. In 1820, he read James 1:5 in the Bible that he could ask God if he needed an answer, so he decided to do that. He saw a vision of God the Father and Jesus Christ, who told Joseph not to join any of the churches. Joseph faced great backlash from others when he tried to share his experience.

SPIRITUAL GUIDING QUESTIONS

Question: What did Joseph notice about the seemingly good feelings between the different religious leaders? Are there people in your life for whom you can practice sincere love instead of "pretended" love? (JS-H 1:6)

Question: When you have struggled with making a choice, what has your process been like? How have you included the Lord in that process, and how might you better include Him in the future? (JS-H 1:10)

Question: While asking God for help might seem simple, how is it a sign of work to sincerely ask God a question? (JS-H 1:11-13)

Question: What have your experiences been like with praying vocally? How can you create more opportunities in the future to pray vocally? (JS-H 1:14)

Question: What are some examples of when you have felt opposition in the midst of trying to do something good? How can you stay true to God, despite opposition and temptations that may arise? (JS-H 1:15-16)

Question: What "power" is unique to the restored gospel of Jesus Christ? What are some blessings you enjoy because of this authorized power? (JS-H 1:19)

Question: Has someone ever minimized a spiritual experience that you had? How can you better anchor your spiritual memories so that they don't become swayed by the opinions of others? (JS-H 1:21-22)

ADDITIONAL THOUGHTS AND NOTES

D&C 2; JOSEPH SMITH-HISTORY 1:27-65

"There Could Not Be a Happier People"

BIG PICTURE

How to feel confident fitting in this week's readings with the entire Doctrine & Covenants

General Context:

- **This week, we focus on the coming forth of the Book of Mormon:**
  - **Section 2** is chronologically the first section in the Doctrine and Covenants, and includes 3 verses that the Angel Moroni quoted to Joseph Smith the first time he appeared to Joseph. (The verses he is quoting originally come from Malachi 4:5-6 but are slightly different than what's in the Bible.)
  - **Joseph Smith-History verses 27-65** tell an overview of the story of how Joseph learned about the golden plates and how they ultimately became the Book of Mormon that we know today.
- **What's our timeline like for the events this week?** For reference, Joseph Smith experienced the First Vision in 1820.
  - Three years following the First Vision, on the evening of **September 21, 1823**, the Angel Moroni visited Joseph Smith to tell him about an ancient American record hidden in a hill. Angel Moroni tells Joseph that he will be able to actually get the gold plates 4 years from that exact date.
  - During those 4 years, Joseph worked for a man named Josiah Stoal. It was during this time that Joseph met and married Emma Hale.
  - Sure enough, on **September 21, 1827**, Joseph Smith was able to retrieve the gold plates. He was able to do some translation from December to February.
  - In **February of 1828**, a new friend named Martin Harris said that he took some of Joseph's translations of the characters from the gold plates to New York, where a young professor named Charles Anthon authenticated the letters. However, Anthon rescinded the authentication when learning about the origin of the plates.
- **Why did Angel Moroni appear to Joseph Smith?** Moroni was the final remaining righteous Nephite in around 400 A.D. His father, Mormon, had compiled most of the record on the plates, but Moroni was tasked with finishing the project. This included abridging the Jaredite records into the Book of Ether and writing his own words in the Book of Moroni. Moroni was the last person to touch these records as he buried them in a hillside. About 1400 years later, he was able to appear to 17-year-old Joseph Smith and teach him about this ancient record.

- **There are two specific people Joseph mentions in his history that you might want some more info on:**
  - **Josiah Stoal:** Joseph Smith mentions that he went to work for a man named Josiah Stoal for a while. It was around this time that rumors were floating around of hidden Spanish treasure. Enterprising people were hiring what were commonly referred to as "seers", or people who would use stones to find objects. Joseph had a reputation of being someone who saw visions, and was hired by Josiah Stoal to help look for treasure. Joseph's father didn't want Joseph to do this, and encouraged him to use his abilities to only serve God. Joseph eventually helped to convince Josiah to stop the search, and no treasure was ever found. Rumors started about Joseph being a "money-digger", which is why Joseph wanted to address this accusation and set the record straight in his history.
  - **Charles Anthon:** Martin Harris had met Joseph Smith and started to assist Joseph's endeavors both personally and financially. After Joseph started on the translation of the gold plates, Martin took a trip to the east with some of the characters from the ancient text and their translation. He visited a couple different professionals, eventually meeting with Charles Anthon, a professor at Columbia University in New York. According to Martin Harris, Anthon prepared a paper to authenticate the characters from the gold plates, but ripped it up once he learned that Joseph had received it from an angel. Charles Anthon later confirmed that he met with Martin Harris, but denied that he authenticated the characters. No matter what actually happened, Martin Harris returned to Joseph Smith with full confidence to financially support him throughout the translation process. In verse 65 of Joseph Smith-History, you'll notice Martin Harris quoting Charles Anthon as saying, "I cannot read a sealed book", after Martin Harris told Anthon that most of the record couldn't be read since it was sealed. In Isaiah 29:11, a prophecy states: "a book that is sealed, which men deliver to one that is learned, saying, Read this, I pray thee: and he saith, I cannot; for it is sealed".
- **Remember that Joseph Smith-History is actually a portion of a larger history that Joseph Smith wrote in 1838.** The 75 verses that we have canonized in scripture were originally chosen from Joseph's larger history to share with the world as missionaries took pamphlets to help them spread the gospel. The verses we are reading this week focus on the coming forth of the Book of Mormon, but the first section covers the First Vision, and the final section deals with the Restoration of the priesthood.

Spiritual Themes:

Look for these themes as you read this week! Find examples in the scriptures, and ponder on what these themes can look like in your life.

- **Repetition and Preparation**

- **Persecution against Good Things**

- **The Sealing Power of the Priesthood**

People to Know:

- **Angel Moroni**
  - Moroni lived in the ancient Americas and was the final righteous Nephite prophet around the year 400 A.D. He helped to finish the compilation of the Book of Mormon that his father had started, burying the record in a hillside once complete. Moroni appeared to Joseph Smith in the form of an angel in the year 1823. After instructing Joseph for 4 years, he allowed Joseph to retrieve the plates in 1827. Moroni took the gold plates back after Joseph was done with the translation process.
- **Joseph Smith**
  - Three years after the First Vision in 1820, Joseph learned about gold plates from the Angel Moroni, found them in a nearby hill, and was instructed to return to the same place every year until 1827. Joseph had just married Emma Hale, and Joseph was finally given permission to retrieve the gold plates. Many people tried to steal the plates or harm Joseph, so Joseph and Emma moved from Palmyra to Harmony, Pennsylvania (near Emma's parents). Emma scribed for Joseph as he started the translation process, but soon Martin Harris came and took the position as scribe.
- **Alvin Smith**
  - Alvin was Joseph's older brother. Alvin died at the age of 25 in November 1823, just a couple months following Joseph's initial visit from the Angel Moroni.
- **Emma Hale Smith**
  - Emma met Joseph when he was hired to work near her family farm in Harmony, Pennsylvania. Her parents did not like Joseph, but Emma and Joseph eventually got married and moved in with his parents in Manchester, New York in January of 1827. Emma was the first scribe for Joseph's translation of the Book of Mormon. The pair moved to Harmony, Pennsylvania to escape persecution and to live by Emma's parents. Emma was pregnant but lost her first baby.

- **Martin Harris**
  - Martin was older and wealthier than Joseph. They became good friends while Joseph was waiting for the gold plates. When Joseph needed to move to Harmony, Pennsylvania with his wife to escape the persecution from those trying to steal the plates, Martin gave him $50 as a gift to help get him there. Martin took a copy of some of the characters to scholars in New York, and got confirmation that the characters were reformed Egyptian.

Where are We?

- **Manchester, New York**
  - This is where the Smith family farm was located.
- **Harmony, Pennsylvania**
  - Joseph mentions that Harmony was where Josiah Stoal was located. It was also here that the Hale family lived, and Joseph was assigned to board with the Hales while working for Josiah. After marrying Emma Hale and living in Palmyra for a while, Joseph and Emma returned to Harmony.

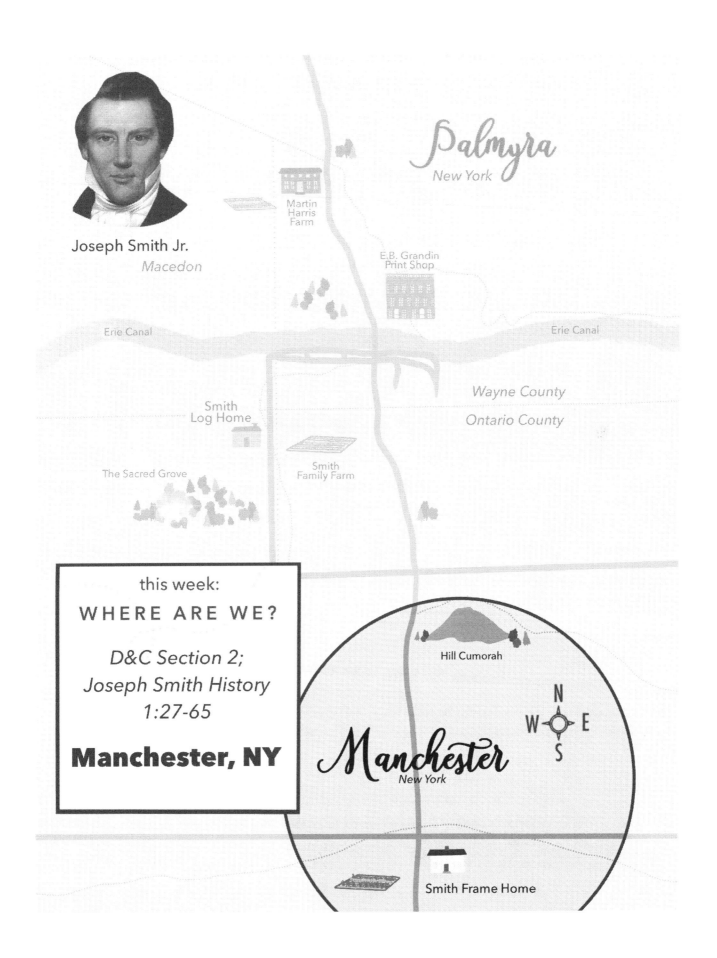

Joseph Smith Jr.
Macedon

Palmyra
New York

Martin Harris Farm

E.B. Grandin Print Shop

Erie Canal

Erie Canal

Smith Log Home

Wayne County

Ontario County

The Sacred Grove

Smith Family Farm

this week:

WHERE ARE WE?

*D&C Section 2;
Joseph Smith History
1:27-65*

Manchester, NY

Hill Cumorah

N
W E
S

Manchester
New York

Smith Frame Home

LITTLE PICTURE

How to understand each section and apply principles to my life

- **D&C 2:**
  - **Revelation Given Through:** Angel Moroni
  - **Revelation Given To:** Joseph Smith
  - **Revelation Given When/Where:** September 1823 in Manchester, New York
  - **Before You Read:** This section includes the words of the Angel Moroni to Joseph Smith. It is a small portion of Joseph Smith's history. Moroni quotes Malachi 4:5-6, with a few little changes in emphasis. This is the earliest revelation, chronologically, in the entire Doctrine and Covenants.
  - **What You'll Read About:** The Lord will reveal priesthood keys through Elijah so the Earth is not wasted at His coming.

- **Joseph Smith-History 1:27-65**

  - **Before You Read:** In earlier verses in this chapter, we learned about Joseph Smith's family, the First Vision, and the backlash that came to him from sharing that experience with others. Three years had passed since the First Vision, and Joseph hadn't received any more heavenly visitors, until the one he describes in these verses. The story in verses 64-65 was prophesied about in Isaiah 29:11-12.
  - **What You'll Read About:** Joseph had been living his life since the First Vision, without any further divine direction. Three years after the First Vision, the Angel Moroni appeared to him while he was praying one night. Moroni told Joseph about golden plates that were buried nearby, and quoted from the Biblical books of Malachi, Isaiah, Acts, and Joel. The angel left, and then returned twice more to repeat the same message, cautioning that Joseph would be tempted to use the plates to get money. Joseph had to get up and work for the day, but was so exhausted that he fainted. Moroni appeared to him again to repeat his message, and instructed Joseph to tell his father what he had seen. Joseph obeyed, and was able to go and discover the plates, although he was told not to retrieve them for four more years. A couple years later in 1825, Joseph worked for Josiah Stoal in Harmony, Pennsylvania and eventually married Emma Hale in 1827. Persecution followed him, so Joseph and Emma went to work on the Smith farm in New York. Joseph was finally able to get the plates in September of 1827, leading to even more persecution. A man named Martin Harris gave them some money so they could travel back to Pennsylvania. Joseph copied some of the characters from the plates, and Martin Harris took a copy of some of the characters to Professor Charles Anthon to have them authenticated. He did so, but when he heard where they came from, the professor tore up the certificate.

SPIRITUAL GUIDING QUESTIONS

Question: What is one way your heart has been turned to your ancestors? What blessings have come as you've had your heart turned to ancestors? (D&C 2:2-3)

Question: What is something an ancestor has done that has blessed your life?
(D&C 2:2-3)

Question: Why did Joseph pray in 1823? What do you think he was expecting? How was Angel Moroni's message an answer to Joseph's personal prayer? (JS-H 1:29)

Question: How has the Book of Mormon been a blessing to your life? What are some gospel concepts taught in that book that have brought you closer to the Savior? (JS-H 1:34)

Question: Why do you think Angel Moroni repeated his message so many times? (JS-H 1:44-47)

Question: Why was it helpful for Joseph to be warned about how Satan would try to tempt him? What are some temptations you think you might face in your future, and how could you try to prepare to face those temptations? (JS-H 1:46)

Question: How did Joseph's father support Joseph? How could you show greater support to the people around you? (JS-H 1:48-50)

ADDITIONAL THOUGHTS AND NOTES

D&C 3 - 5

"My Work Shall Go Forth"

BIG PICTURE

How to feel confident fitting in this week's readings with the entire Doctrine & Covenants

General Context:

- **This week's readings center around the loss of 116 pages of manuscript of the Book of Mormon:**
  - **Section 3 (July 1828)** covers the Lord's reprimand to Joseph directly following the loss of the manuscript pages in the summer of 1828.
  - **Section 4 (Feb 1829)** is when Joseph's father came to check on the wellbeing of Joseph and Emma about 7 months after the manuscript loss, and then asked for a revelation to hear the will of God in his own life.
  - **Section 5 (Mar 1829)** includes the Lord's directions to Joseph that Martin Harris can be one of the Three Witnesses as long as he repents and humbles himself.
- **What was actually lost?** Martin Harris's wife was concerned that Joseph was conning Martin out of money. She was demanding some sort of proof that Joseph really had gold plates. Martin asked Joseph multiple times for some manuscript pages to show his wife. Despite the Lord telling Joseph to not do this, Joseph did, and the pages were lost. We don't know exactly what happened to these lost pages, although Martin made it clear that he looked everywhere in his home and on his farm, but could not locate them. Joseph said that on these 116 pages of manuscripts, he had translated the Book of Lehi. This was an abridgement by the prophet Mormon from what Joseph called the plates of Lehi.
  - **We actually know a lot of what Lehi probably wrote about in his record!** This is because Nephi, Lehi's son and the first author in the Book of Mormon as we have it today, wrote about some of the same events and teachings that he knew his dad had written in his own record, too. However, it's interesting to note that Joseph had not translated Nephi's record yet, so he didn't know that Nephi had included a lot of information from Lehi's record.
  - **Remember: Martin Harris lost the manuscript pages, not any portion of the golden plates.** This means that Joseph still had the original writings from the Book of Lehi in the gold plates, and he could have just translated them again. However, the Lord told Joseph not to do this.

- **This was actually a very dark period of time for Joseph and Emma Smith.** As you might imagine, Joseph disobeying the Lord and allowing Martin to take and lose the manuscript pages really negatively affected Joseph. He lost his ability to translate for many months. But what adds to the heartbreak is that around this exact same time, Emma and Joseph's first son was born and died on June 15, 1828.

- **Does D&C 4 sound familiar to you?** I'm going to venture a guess that if you served a full-time mission, you have read, studied, and possibly even memorized the seven verses in this section. This section beautifully summarizes why sharing the gospel of Jesus Christ is important. It's interesting to note, though, that Joseph Smith received this revelation for his father, who never served a full-time mission. Joseph's father had come to check in on Joseph and Emma in Harmony in February of 1829, several months after their devastating losses of a child, the manuscript pages, and Joseph's ability to translate. Joseph Smith Sr. actually found the Smiths in good spirits, and he asked his son to receive a revelation from the Lord so that Joseph Sr. would know his purpose. Joseph received the words in D&C 4 for his father. This revelation became pivotal for Joseph Smith Sr., as he had felt very protective of his son's divine mission up to that point, choosing to not discuss it with too many people to avoid bringing unnecessary persecution. However, from this point forward, he began to share the gospel more openly, ultimately opening doors to help his son move the work of the Lord forward.

Spiritual Themes:

Look for these themes as you read this week! Find examples in the scriptures, and ponder on what these themes can look like in your life.

- **Trusting God More than Man**

- **Desiring to Serve God**

- **God's Plan Cannot be Stopped**

People to Know:

- **Martin Harris**
  - Martin was older and wealthier than Joseph. They became good friends while Joseph was waiting for the gold plates. When Joseph needed to move to Harmony, Pennsylvania with Emma to escape the persecution and those trying to steal the plates, Martin gave him $50 as a gift to help get him there.
  - Martin took a copy of some of the characters to scholars in New York, and got confirmation that the characters were reformed Egyptian.

- Martin followed Joseph to Harmony, and took over for Emma as Joseph's scribe. Martin's wife, Lucy, also stayed with them for a bit, but was skeptical that Joseph never showed anyone the plates.
- Martin wanted to show his wife some of the transcriptions so that she would be pleased that he was investing money in the cause, and asked Joseph for some of the manuscript pages. After being given some pages, he lost them, and felt great remorse when he had to tell Joseph.
- After spending some time in Palmyra, Martin went and visited Joseph in Harmony to see how he was doing. He was delighted that Joseph had been forgiven by the Lord and was preparing to start translating again. Joseph received a revelation in March 1829 that told Martin to believe Joseph's testimony, and confirmed that Martin could be a witness to the Book of Mormon at some point.
- **Joseph Smith Sr.**
  - He was a very supportive father to Joseph, and was the first person that he told about many of the visions he experienced while growing up. He supported Joseph in keeping the plates hidden after he had obtained them.
  - After the fiasco with Martin Harris and the lost manuscript pages, Joseph Sr. was concerned about his son's well-being. He knew Joseph Jr. had lost the ability to translate for a while, and was concerned that he wasn't hearing from him as often. He went to visit Joseph Jr. in Harmony, Pennsylvania.
  - While Joseph Sr. was in Harmony, discovering that his son was doing fine again, Joseph Jr. received a revelation for his father. This revelation in February 1829 spoke about Joseph Sr.'s desires and his qualification to do missionary work.
- **Joseph Smith Jr.**
  - Joseph retrieved the gold plates in 1827, the same year that he married Emma Hale. Joseph and Emma moved from New York to Harmony, Pennsylvania in order to escape persecution and focus on translating the gold plates. Emma was pregnant with their first child.
  - Emma scribed for Joseph, but soon Martin Harris came and took over as the new scribe. To appease Martin's hesitant wife, Martin asked for some pages of translated manuscript to show her. Unfortunately, Martin lost the manuscript pages, and remorsefully admitted to Joseph what had happened.
  - Joseph received a revelation from the Lord about these lost pages, and subsequently lost his ability to translate for a few months in the summer of 1828.
  - Joseph was living in Harmony still when both his father and Martin Harris visited and received revelations.

Where are We?

- **Harmony, Pennsylvania**
  - Emma Hale Smith's family lived in Harmony.
  - Following Joseph and Emma's successful retrieval of the gold plates, persecution in Manchester became so great that Emma and Joseph decided to move to be near her parents in Harmony.
  - Emma scribed for Joseph here in Harmony until Martin Harris showed up and took over during her pregnancy. Emma lost her newborn baby, and Martin Harris lost the manuscript pages at around the same time, so Emma and Joseph mourned over both losses here in late 1828.
  - By early 1829, the translation was back on. Eventually, Oliver Cowdery showed up and offered to be Joseph's new scribe. They received many revelations together here, and the Aaronic priesthood was restored in the nearby woods.

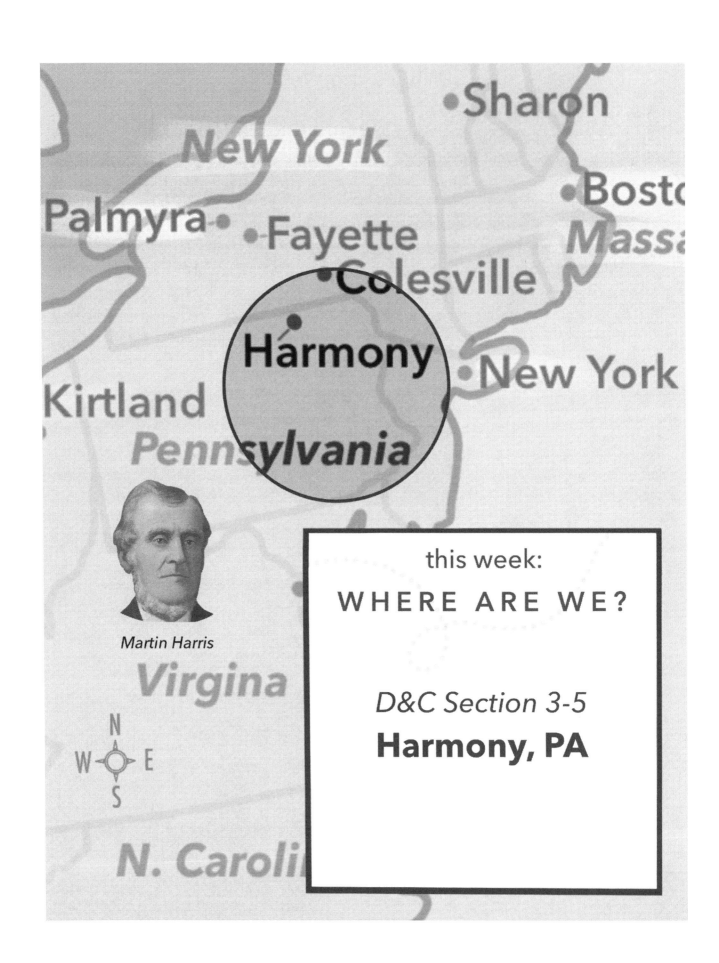

Sharon

New York

Palmyra • • Fayette

• Colesville

Boston

Massa

Harmony

New York

Kirtland

Pennsylvania

Martin Harris

Virgina

N
W — E
S

N. Caroli

this week:

WHERE ARE WE?

D&C Section 3-5
Harmony, PA

LITTLE PICTURE

How to understand each section and apply principles to my life

- **D&C 3:**
  - **Revelation Given Through:** Joseph Smith
  - **Revelation Given To:** Joseph Smith
  - **Revelation Given When/Where:** July 1828 in Harmony, Pennsylvania
  - **Before You Read:** This revelation was given to Joseph Smith after the loss of the 116 manuscript pages of the Book of Mormon.
  - **What You'll Read About:** The Lord declares that the designs of God will not be frustrated, and that we should not fear men more than we fear God. The Lord says that He has chosen Joseph, but Joseph can still fall because of transgression. The Book of Mormon will still come forward, and the Lord shares the purpose for the book.

- **D&C 4:**
  - **Revelation Given Through:** Joseph Smith
  - **Revelation Given To:** Joseph Smith Sr.
  - **Revelation Given When/Where:** February 1829 in Harmony, Pennsylvania
  - **Before You Read:** Joseph Smith Sr. visited his son in Pennsylvania to offer his support. While he was there, he asked his son for a revelation to know what the Lord wanted him to do.
  - **What You'll Read About:** In this great missionary revelation, the Lord talks about our desires and the qualifications to do God's work.

- **D&C 5:**
  - **Revelation Given Through:** Joseph Smith
  - **Revelation Given To:** Martin Harris and Joseph Smith
  - **Revelation Given When/Where:** March 1829 in Harmony, Pennsylvania
  - **Before You Read:** After the debacle with the 116 pages, Martin Harris once again visited Joseph Smith. While he was there, Joseph received this revelation.
  - **What You'll Read About:** Martin is told to believe Joseph Smith's testimony, because the Lord has given Joseph the gift of translation. The Lord tells Joseph He will choose witnesses to testify to the world of the Book of Mormon. If Martin remains humble, he will be one of those witnesses. Joseph is to pause the translation process after a few more pages and wait for the Lord's instructions.

SPIRITUAL GUIDING QUESTIONS

Question: What natural consequence was Joseph Smith given after his transgression? How do you see the natural consequences of sin in your life? (D&C 3:9-15)

Question: What do you fear more right now: the judgments of men, or the judgments of God? When have you felt both? (D&C 3:7)

Question: How can we possibly stand blameless before God at the last day? What could you reasonably do right now in order to achieve that? (D&C 4:2)

Question: Do you desire to serve God and perform missionary work? How can you continue to grow that desire? (D&C 4:3)

Question: Which Christlike qualities was Joseph Smith Sr. told were most important? Which of these qualities come naturally to you? Which of these qualities will take more work to develop? (D&C 4:5-6)

Question: What did the Lord ask Martin to do before receiving his witness? How can we follow this same pattern? (D&C 5:17, 24, 28)

Question: What does it look like to stop and stand still while trusting in the Lord? How can you create more stillness in your life right now? (D&C 5:34)

ADDITIONAL THOUGHTS AND NOTES

D&C 6 - 9

"This Is the Spirit of Revelation"

BIG PICTURE

How to feel confident fitting in this week's readings with the entire Doctrine & Covenants

General Context:

- **Someone new to our story of the Restoration enters as the main character for our reading this week: Oliver Cowdery!** You'll notice that all of these sections take place in the same exact month: **April of 1829.**
  - **Section 6** is directed to Oliver as he begins his position as Joseph's new scribe.
  - **Section 7** reveals that the apostle John desired to stay on the earth until Jesus Christ's return.
  - **Section 8** includes the Lord giving Oliver permission to attempt to translate the plates.
  - **Section 9** revokes that permission, although the Lord makes it clear that Oliver is not condemned for trying to translate.
- **Joseph needed a new scribe.** The summer of 1828 is when Martin Harris lost the 116 pages of manuscript, and Joseph temporarily lost his ability to translate the gold plates. Last week, we saw that a few months after that, Joseph was given his gift back, and he was ready to start translating again. But who would be his scribe?
- **A young school teacher named Oliver Cowdery had just moved in with the Joseph Smith Sr. and Lucy Mack Smith family in Manchester, New York.** Remember what Joseph Smith Sr. had been taught in D&C 4? The Lord's revelation for Joseph Sr. inspired him to tell their houseguest, Oliver, about Joseph's visions and golden plates. Oliver considered himself an honest seeker of truth, and he naturally became very curious. Oliver told his good friend David Whitmer that he was going to try and figure out whether Joseph was telling the truth. As he pondered and studied, Oliver received a private and serious spiritual revelation that helped him know that he should become Joseph's new scribe. (When you read D&C 6, you'll notice the Lord referring to this spiritual experience!) After the school year was done, he went with Joseph's brother Samuel Smith to Harmony, Pennsylvania. On the way there, Oliver stopped by David Whitmer's family home to tell him he was going to meet Joseph. Oliver showed up in Pennsylvania to help Joseph translate in April 1829, and began working as Joseph's scribe on April 7.

Spiritual Themes:

Look for these themes as you read this week! Find examples in the scriptures, and ponder on what these themes can look like in your life.

- **Patterns of Receiving Personal Revelation**

- **Remembering and Trusting Past Spiritual Experiences**

- **Righteous Desires are Known to the Lord**

People to Know:

- **Oliver Cowdery**
  - Oliver Cowdery was a young school teacher who lived at the Smith family home in Manchester, after Joseph and Emma had already moved out to Harmony. Oliver learned about Joseph's visions and golden plates, and naturally became very curious. He told his good friend David Whitmer that he was going to try and figure out whether Joseph was telling the truth.
  - Oliver received a private and serious spiritual revelation that helped him know that he should become Joseph's new scribe. After the school year was done, he went with Samuel Smith to Harmony, Pennsylvania, and stopped by David Whitmer's family home to tell him he was going to meet Joseph.
  - Oliver showed up in Pennsylvania to help Joseph translate in April 1829, and was given a revelation about inquiring in faith. Oliver began as Joseph's scribe.
  - That same month, Oliver and Joseph received revelations about John the Beloved, Oliver's desire to translate the plates, and the Lord's command to Oliver to have patience with his current assignment as scribe.
- **Joseph Smith**
  - Joseph and Emma were living in Harmony, Pennsylvania. After just enduring several dark months following the loss of their first child, and the loss of the 116 pages of manuscript, Joseph had fully repented and was ready to begin translating again.
  - A man named Oliver Cowdery had become good friends with his mother, father, and family. Oliver eventually came to Joseph and volunteered to be his new scribe. Joseph received confirmation of this, and the pair started to work together to translate and scribe more pages of the Book of Mormon in April of 1829.

Where are We?

- **Harmony, Pennsylvania**
  - Emma Hale Smith's family lived in Harmony.
  - Following Joseph and Emma's successful retrieval of the gold plates, persecution in Manchester became so great that Emma and Joseph decided to move to be near her parents in Harmony.
  - Emma scribed for Joseph here in Harmony until Martin Harris showed up and took over during her pregnancy. Emma lost her newborn baby, and Martin Harris lost the manuscript pages at around the same time, so Emma and Joseph mourned together over both losses here in late 1828.
  - By early 1829, the translation was back on. Eventually, Oliver Cowdery showed up and offered to be Joseph's new scribe. They received many revelations together here, and the Aaronic priesthood was restored in the nearby woods.

New York

Palmyra

Manchester

Fayette

Finger Lakes

South Bainbridge

Colesville

Susquehanna River

Harmony

N

W   E

S

Pennsylvania

Susquehanna River

this week:

WHERE ARE WE?

D&C Section 6-9
Harmony, PA

Oliver Cowdry

LITTLE PICTURE

How to understand each section and apply principles to my life

- **D&C 6:**
  - **Revelation Given Through:** Joseph Smith
  - **Revelation Given To:** Oliver Cowdery
  - **Revelation Given When/Where:** April 1829 in Harmony, Pennsylvania
  - **Before You Read:** Oliver Cowdery, a schoolteacher, had heard of Joseph Smith's visions and gold plates. Oliver had prayed and received a confirmation of their truthfulness, then traveled to Pennsylvania to meet Joseph Smith. Oliver soon became a scribe for Joseph in the translation process, and this revelation was given through the Urim and Thummim to Oliver.
  - **What You'll Read About:** The Lord teaches that if we have a desire, we are called to the work. He reminds Oliver of the answer he had previously received, and commands him to stand by Joseph with patience and faith. The Lord says that Oliver can receive the gift of translation if he desires, and that he and Joseph would be witnesses to others. He counsels Oliver not to fear, but to believe and sin no more.

- **D&C 7:**
  - **Revelation Given Through:** Joseph Smith
  - **Revelation Given To:** Joseph Smith and Oliver Cowdery
  - **Revelation Given When/Where:** April 1829 in Harmony, Pennsylvania
  - **Before You Read:** Joseph and Oliver were wondering what had happened to the apostle John. Joseph saw a parchment in a vision and translated it with the Urim and Thummim.
  - **What You'll Read About:** We hear from the apostle John's perspective that the Lord granted his desire to stay on the earth until Christ's second coming. Christ gave Peter, James, and John the keys of the gospel ministry.

- **D&C 8:**
  - **Revelation Given Through:** Joseph Smith
  - **Revelation Given To:** Oliver Cowdery
  - **Revelation Given When/Where:** April 1829 in Harmony, Pennsylvania
  - **Before You Read:** Oliver Cowdery wanted to translate the plates. Joseph asked the Lord and received this revelation.
  - **What You'll Read About:** The Lord grants Oliver's request and explains to him one of the ways that inspiration is received. He counsels Oliver to apply himself to his new gift, and teaches that he has many gifts. Spiritual knowledge and gifts come to us through faith.

- **D&C 9:**
  - **Revelation Given Through:** Joseph Smith
  - **Revelation Given To:** Oliver Cowdery
  - **Revelation Given When/Where:** April 1829 in Harmony, Pennsylvania
  - **Before You Read:** While we don't have any details of what exactly happened, apparently Oliver Cowdery's attempt to translate the Book of Mormon didn't go very well. Joseph received this revelation.
  - **What You'll Read About:** This revelation revokes Oliver Cowdery's permission to translate, and reiterates his job as scribe while Joseph translates. The Lord counsels Oliver that he needs to study and ask in order to receive revelation, but He also reminds Oliver that he is not condemned.

SPIRITUAL GUIDING QUESTIONS

Question: Why is it sometimes difficult to trust our past spiritual experiences? When is a time you had to rely on your memory of a previously answered prayer instead of receiving constant reassurance? (D&C 6:22-23)

Question: What are some ways you could reasonably look unto the Lord in every thought? How could you work to improve how often you do this? (D&C 6:36)

Question: How can we find joy in doing different things than those around us? (D&C 7:4-5)

Question: According to the section heading, why did Joseph Smith and Oliver Cowdery even receive this revelation? What can we learn from this? (D&C 7 section heading)

Question: Which way to receive inspiration does the Lord teach Oliver about? Have you received personal revelation in this way before? (D&C 8:2-3)

Question: What does the Lord teach us about asking Him questions? What should we do before asking questions? (D&C 9:7-8)

Question: Have you felt a stupor of thought or a burning in your bosom before as part of your process of receiving personal revelation? How can you become even more sensitive to these spiritual responses? (D&C 9:8-9)

ADDITIONAL THOUGHTS AND NOTES

D&C 10 - 11

"That You May Come Off Conqueror"

BIG PICTURE

How to feel confident fitting in this week's readings with the entire Doctrine & Covenants

General Context:

- **This week, we need to officially finish up learning how Joseph dealt with the lost manuscript pages and whether or not he should re-translate that portion.**
    - **Section 10** (April 1829) is a longer section that includes the Lord's specific directions to Joseph to NOT re-translate the portion of the plates whose translation had been lost and warns about Satan's plans.
    - **Section 11** (May 1829) is a revelation Joseph received on behalf of his brother Hyrum, telling Hyrum to prepare to serve a mission.
- **We are virtually in the same exact timeframe as we were last week:** the spring of 1829 at Joseph and Emma's home in Harmony, Pennsylvania. You'll remember that Oliver Cowdery had just traveled from the Smith home in Manchester to meet Joseph and begin work as his scribe. The translation process was back on in full-swing, which made the question even more pressing: Should Joseph go back and re-translate the portion that had been lost?
- **A quick reminder (and checkout D&C 3 for even more!)** that in order to let Martin Harris appease his wife's concerns about whether or not Joseph was telling the truth, Joseph let Martin Harris take 116 pages of manuscript. Martin lost all 116 of these pages, Joseph was devastated, the Lord reprimanded Joseph, and Joseph lost his ability to translate for a while. But even though the manuscript pages were lost, the original records on the gold plates were still there. Joseph could have just gone back and translated those particular pages again.
- **However, the Lord warned Joseph that there was a plan in place to try to discredit him.** Evil men had gotten those 116 manuscript pages and had made slight alterations. Their plan was to use these altered pages to "prove" that Joseph was making everything up once Joseph released the re-translated portions. This seems like absolutely devastating news to Joseph, since the world wouldn't ever get what was on those 116 pages.

- **The good news is that Nephi and Mormon, hundreds and hundreds of years prior to this moment, had been prepared by the Lord to help bridge the gap left by missing manuscripts.** Joseph said that the portion he had translated and then lost covered the Book of Lehi, which contained stories and teachings from the prophet Lehi that were then abridged by Mormon when Mormon was compiling all the records. Both Nephi (1 Nephi 9:5) and Mormon (Words of Mormon 1:3-7) were inspired by the Lord to include what seemed to them like repetition in their records. Nephi felt inspired to make a summary (abridgment) of what he knew his father had already written and include it in his own records. And Mormon felt inspired to include Nephi's summary AND the Book of Lehi, even though they said similar things. While we still don't have the original words from the Book of Lehi to study out of today, we can be confident that the Lord made sure we have the stories, teachings, and doctrine that we need right now.
- **What has Hyrum been up to?** Hyrum was 5 years older than his brother Joseph. Hyrum was by far the most educated of the Smith children, and he served on the Palmyra school board. Part of his job was to interview teachers, including the traveling schoolteacher Oliver Cowdery. By 1829, Joseph was living in Harmony, Pennsylvania. The teacher Oliver Cowdery had traveled to Joseph to become his scribe. It is at this time that Hyrum traveled to Harmony, too. Hyrum wanted to know of his standing and purpose before the Lord, so Joseph received the revelation known as D&C 11 on Hyrum's behalf. Part of this section includes direction for Hyrum to prepare to serve a mission. Hyrum served several missions and ended up being a major leader in establishing the Lord's restored Church.

Spiritual Themes:

Look for these themes as you read this week! Find examples in the scriptures, and ponder on what these themes can look like in your life.

- **God's Will Always Prevails**

- **The Strategies of Satan**

- **Studying God's Word**

People to Know:

- **Hyrum Smith**
  - Hyrum was Joseph's older brother. After Oliver Cowdery had joined Joseph to help in transcription, and after Hyrum's younger brother Samuel had become converted, Hyrum also traveled from New York to Harmony, Pennsylvania. In May 1829, Hyrum asked Joseph for a revelation on his behalf, and Joseph received revelation about how Hyrum should gain knowledge to prepare for a future mission call.

- **Joseph Smith**
  - Living in Harmony, Pennsylvania with his wife Emma, Joseph was beginning the translation process again. Oliver Cowdery, a schoolteacher, had volunteered to be Joseph's new scribe. Joseph's father had previously visited Joseph and received a revelation with specific directions for him. Joseph's brother, Hyrum, had now travelled to Joseph and wanted to receive his own personal direction from the Lord.

Where are We?

- **Harmony, Pennsylvania**
  - Emma Hale Smith's family lived in Harmony.
  - Following Joseph and Emma's successful retrieval of the gold plates, persecution in Manchester became so great that Emma and Joseph decided to move to be near her parents in Harmony.
  - Emma scribed for Joseph here in Harmony until Martin Harris showed up and took over during her pregnancy. Emma lost her newborn baby, and Martin Harris lost the manuscript pages at around the same time, so Emma and Joseph mourned together over both losses here in late 1828.
  - By early 1829, the translation was back on. Eventually, Oliver Cowdery showed up and offered to be Joseph's new scribe. They received many revelations together here, and the Aaronic priesthood was restored in the nearby woods.

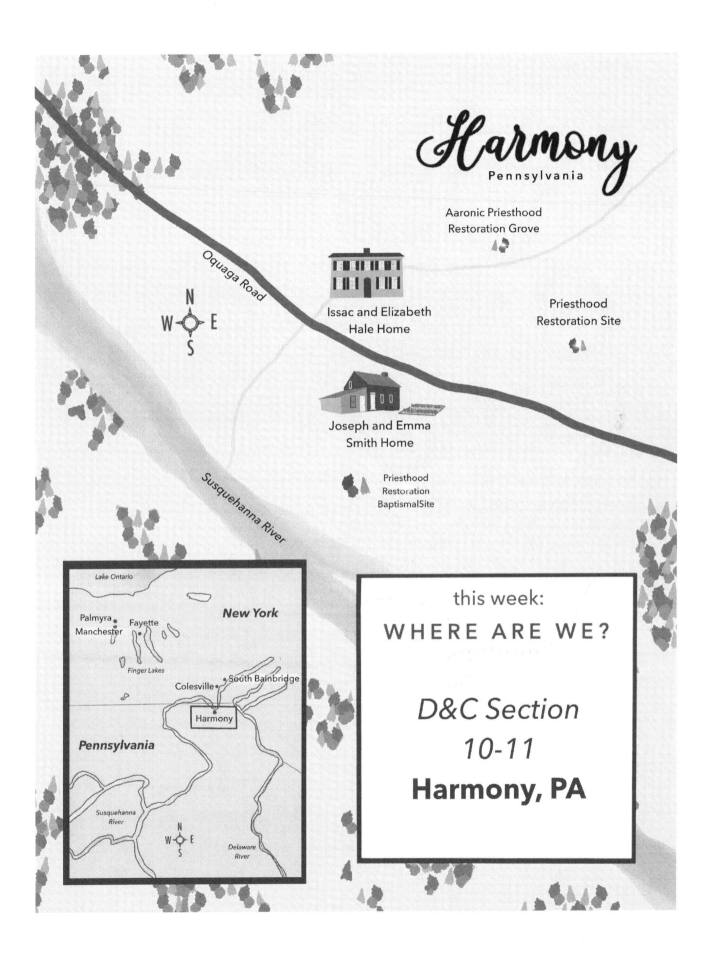

Harmony
Pennsylvania

Aaronic Priesthood
Restoration Grove

Priesthood
Restoration Site

Oquaga Road

Issac and Elizabeth
Hale Home

Joseph and Emma
Smith Home

Priesthood
Restoration
BaptismalSite

Susquehanna River

Lake Ontario

New York

Palmyra
Manchester   Fayette

Finger Lakes

Colesville • South Bainbridge

Pennsylvania

Harmony

Susquehanna
River

Delaware
River

this week:

WHERE ARE WE?

*D&C Section
10-11*

Harmony, PA

LITTLE PICTURE

How to understand each section and apply principles to my life

- **D&C 10:**
    - **Revelation Given Through:** Joseph Smith
    - **Revelation Given To:** Joseph Smith
    - **Revelation Given When/Where:** April 1829 in Harmony, Pennsylvania
    - **Before You Read:** Joseph and Oliver were wondering whether they should retranslate a portion of the Book of Mormon. We read about the first part of this story in D&C 3, when Martin Harris lost the 116 pages manuscript of translated pages in the Book of Mormon.
    - **What You'll Read About:** This revelation reveals what wicked men are going to do with the 116 lost manuscript pages of the Book of Mormon, and instructs Joseph not to re-translate. Satan stirs up the wicked and corrupts their hearts to try to destroy the work of God. The Lord tells them to translate the books of Nephi through Mosiah. Christ testifies of Himself, and of His own power and doctrine.

- **D&C 11:**
    - **Revelation Given Through:** Joseph Smith
    - **Revelation Given To:** Hyrum Smith
    - **Revelation Given When/Where:** May 1829 in Harmony, Pennsylvania
    - **Before You Read:** Hyrum visited Joseph in Pennsylvania and Joseph received this revelation.
    - **What You'll Read About:** The Lord again declares that the field is ready to harvest, and a marvelous work will soon come forth. He commands Hyrum to seek wisdom and preach repentance, and teaches Hyrum that his mind will be enlightened through the Spirit. Hyrum is told to obtain God's word so that he can be effective in proclaiming the gospel when the time comes. All who desire are called to work in the Lord's vineyard.

SPIRITUAL GUIDING QUESTIONS

Question: What blessings are we promised when we pray always? Have you seen this blessing in your life? (D&C 10:5)

Question: What do we learn about how Satan works? What patterns and strategies does he use? Which strategies can you see him using currently? (D&C 10:8-29)

Question: What should we be seeking first? How can we make sure our priorities are in the correct order? (D&C 11:7, 21)

Question: Where should we put our trust? How have you practiced this, especially when life becomes unsure? (D&C 11:12)

Question: How does the Lord enlighten our minds? What experiences have you had where you felt your mind was enlightened? (D&C 11:13)

Question: What is Hyrum told to do while he waits for an official call to preach? How can we gather knowledge and doctrine while waiting for bigger assignments? (D&C 11:15-22)

Question: What sources of learning have helped you become the most familiar with Christ's doctrine throughout your life? (D&C 11:16)

ADDITIONAL THOUGHTS AND NOTES

D&C 12 - 17; JOSEPH SMITH-HISTORY 1:66-75

"Upon You My Fellow Servants"

BIG PICTURE

How to feel confident fitting in this week's readings with the entire Doctrine & Covenants

General Context:

- **This week, there are two big focuses: The Restoration of the Aaronic priesthood in Harmony, and the selection of the Three Witnesses in Fayette, New York.** This is what we will study:
  - **Section 12** (May 1829) is a revelation to Joseph Knight Sr.
  - **Section 13** (May 1829) is the Restoration of the Aaronic priesthood. John the Baptist spoke these words to Joseph and Oliver Cowdery.
  - **Joseph Smith-History 1:66-75** includes the narration around the events of the Restoration of the Aaronic priesthood in May of 1829.
  - **Section 14** (June 1829) is a revelation to David Whitmer.
  - **Section 15** (June 1829) is a revelation to John Whitmer
  - **Section 16** (June 1829) is a revelation to Peter Whitmer Jr.
  - **Section 17** (June 1829) is a revelation confirming that Martin Harris, Oliver Cowdery, and David Whitmer should be the Three Witnesses to the Book of Mormon.
- **We start off in Harmony, which is where Joseph and Emma had been living for over a year.** This is where Martin Harris first helped scribe for Joseph, where the Smiths had to endure some dark times with the loss of their first child and the loss of Joseph's ability to translate, and where Oliver Cowdery had recently joined Joseph to continue in the translation process. Oliver and Joseph had questions about baptism and went to pray about it. On May 15, 1829, John the Baptist appeared to Joseph Smith and Oliver Cowdery and restored the Aaronic priesthood to these two men. They were instructed to then baptize each other, and told that the greater Melchizidek priesthood would be given to them at a later time.
  - **Who is Joseph Knight Sr.?** While still in Harmony, Joseph was visited by a man named Joseph Knight, who he already knew very well. Joseph Knight Sr. had previously hired Joseph Smith to work on his farm, and ultimately became a great friend to the Smith family. He was even present when Joseph arrived home after obtaining the gold plates in 1827. The Knight family lived in nearby Colesville, New York. Joseph Knight sent some supplies and money to Joseph and Emma while they were translating the plates in Harmony. When Joseph Knight came to visit Joseph in Harmony, he asked for a personal revelation and Joseph received the words as recorded in D&C 12.

- **There is a big transition in this week's reading to focus on a new family and a new location that will become super important as the Restoration rolls on: The Whitmer family in Fayette, New York.** Peter Whitmer Sr. owned a farm here, and many of his children lived with them. Peter's son, David, became good friends with Oliver Cowdery when Oliver was teaching, and Oliver stopped by their house on his way to meet Joseph for the first time in Harmony. David and his family started to become interested in what Joseph was doing. A few months later, Oliver asked the Whitmer family if he, Joseph, and Emma could move to their home while they finished the Book of Mormon translation due to growing opposition in Harmony. The Whitmer family was extremely welcoming with allowing Joseph, Emma, and Oliver to come to Fayette, and it was actually here that the Book of Mormon translation was completed.
    - **Three of the Whitmer sons** asked Joseph for personal revelations during this time, which is where D&C 14, 15, and 16 come from.
    - It was also here at the Whitmer farm that Oliver Cowdery, David Whitmer, and Martin Harris became the **Three Witnesses to the Book of Mormon.**

Spiritual Themes:

Look for these themes as you read this week! Find examples in the scriptures, and ponder on what these themes can look like in your life.

- **Importance of the Aaronic Priesthood**

- **God's Usage of Witnesses**

- **Our Righteous Desires Matter**

People to Know:

- **Joseph Knight Sr.**
    - Joseph Knight Sr. hired Joseph Smith to work on his farm, and ultimately became a great friend to the Smith family. He was even present when Joseph arrived home after obtaining the gold plates. The Knight family lived in Colesville, New York.
    - Joseph Knight sent some supplies and money to Joseph and Emma while they were translating the plates in Harmony. Joseph received a revelation for Joseph Knight in May 1829.

- **Oliver Cowdery**
  - Oliver Cowdery had been a young school teacher who lived at the Smith family home in Manchester. After learning about Joseph's vision and gold plates, he traveled to Harmony and ultimately became Joseph's scribe. Joseph and Oliver received the Aaronic priesthood together.
  - When persecution in Harmony became too much, Oliver reached out to his friend David Whitmer, and asked if David's parents, Peter and Mary, would host Joseph, Emma, and Oliver as they finished the Book of Mormon translation. They agreed, and the three of them moved to the Whitmer home in Fayette, New York.
  - After the completion of the translation in the Whitmer home, Oliver, David, and Martin Harris had a desire to become one of the Three Witnesses to the gold plates. Oliver was officially called to be one of the Three Witnesses in June 1829 and saw an angel, along with the plates and other relics.
- **David Whitmer**
  - David became a good friend of Oliver Cowdery's while visiting Palmyra as Oliver was teaching. Both David and Oliver were curious about Joseph Smith, and Oliver wrote to David many times to tell him about his desires to go help Joseph, and what the translation process was like after Oliver had arrived in Harmony.
  - David lived in Fayette, New York with his parents, Peter and Mary, and many siblings. When Oliver wrote to David, asking if his family could host Joseph, Emma, and Oliver as they finished the translation, David helped make that happen. He even experienced a miracle where his farm duties were partially completed, allowing him to help Joseph and Emma sooner than planned. David asked Joseph for a revelation once he was residing in their home in June 1829, and Joseph received one for him.
  - David was moved with a righteous desire to be one of the Three Witnesses of the Book of Mormon, and was officially called to be one of them, seeing the plates in June 1829.
- **John Whitmer**
  - John was David Whitmer's brother, also a son of Peter and Mary. Joseph stayed at John's father's residence in Fayette, New York to finish the translation of the Book of Mormon.
  - John asked Joseph for a revelation while Joseph was at their home translating in June of 1829, and was given what is considered to be one of the most personal revelations, revealing that the Lord knew he had been asking for what would be the most worthwhile thing to do.
- **Peter Whitmer Jr.**
  - Peter was David Whitmer's brother, and the son of Peter Sr. and Mary. Joseph stayed at his father's residence to finish the translation of the plates. While there, in June of 1829, Peter asked Joseph for a revelation, and was given a similar revelation to his brother, John.

- **Martin Harris**
  - Martin was older and wealthier than Joseph. They became good friends while Joseph was waiting for the gold plates.
  - Martin took a copy of some of the characters to scholars in New York, and got confirmation that the characters were reformed Egyptian.
  - Martin helped Joseph scribe for a short period of time during the translation process, but stopped this role once Martin lost the 116 manuscript pages.
  - A few months later, and with a strong desire to be one of the Three Witnesses, he was called to be one, along with Oliver Cowdery and David Whitmer. Although Martin originally felt he wasn't worthy to see the plates, he was a witness in June 1829.
- **Joseph Smith**
  - Joseph and Emma were living in Harmony, Pennsylvania as the work of the translation of the Book of Mormon continued with Oliver Cowdery. Following the Restoration of the Aaronic priesthood in May 1829, persecution in Harmony started to become too hostile. Oliver asked his friend David Whitmer if his family would open up their home.
  - Joseph, Emma, and Oliver moved to Fayette, New York to stay with the Whitmer family. It is here that Joseph completed his translation of the Book of Mormon. He also received confirmation that Oliver Cowdery, David Whitmer, and Martin Harris were to be the Three Witnesses.

Where are We?

- **Harmony, Pennsylvania**
  - Emma Hale Smith's family lived in Harmony. Joseph and Emma first moved to Harmony after their marriage and mounting persecution in Manchester. During their time in Harmony, Emma, Martin Harris, and Oliver Cowdery scribed for Joseph. This is where the Aaronic priesthood was restored to Joseph and Oliver in May 1829. However, persecution in Harmony was growing to be too much, and Joseph, Emma, and Oliver moved to Fayette to stay with the Whitmers. They kept their home and farm in Harmony, returning from time to time throughout 1830 to tend to the farm, and take care of other business.
- **Fayette, NY**
  - This is where the Whitmer family lived. Peter Whitmer Sr. owned a farm here, and many of his children lived with them. His son, David, became good friends with Oliver Cowdery, and Oliver stopped by their house on his way to go meet Joseph for the first time in Harmony. A few months later, Oliver asked the Whitmer family if he, Joseph, and Emma could move to their home while they finished the Book of Mormon translation, due to growing opposition in Harmony.
  - The Book of Mormon translation was completed here at the Whitmer home in the summer of 1829, and Joseph received revelations for three of the Whitmer sons.
  - It was here that Oliver, Martin, and David became the Three Witnesses to the Book of Mormon, and learned about the future organization of the Church.

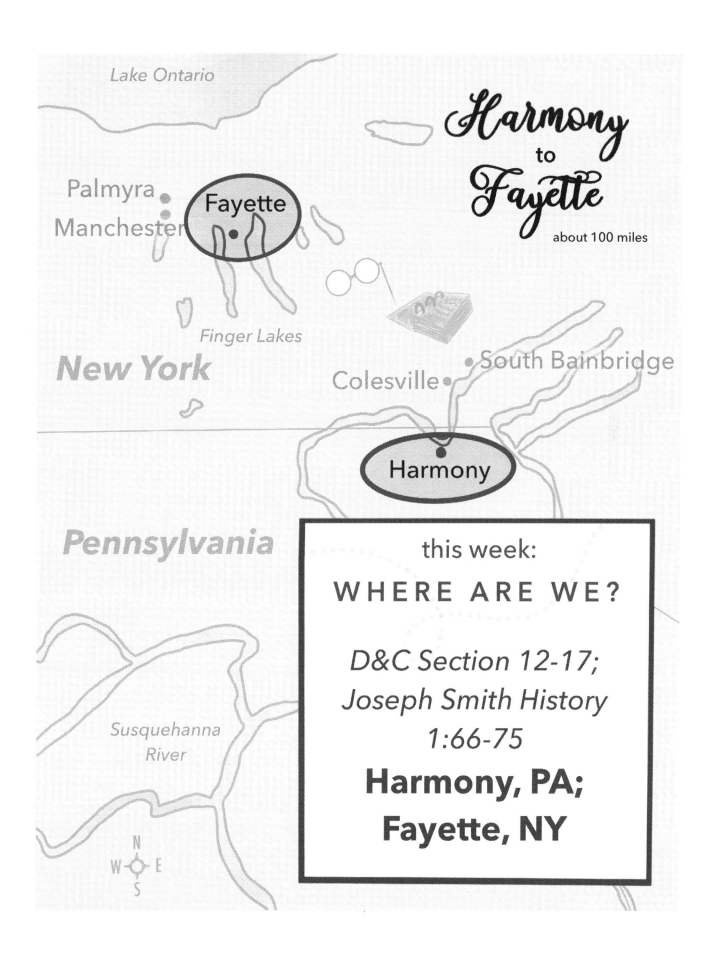

Lake Ontario

Harmony to *Fayette*

about 100 miles

Palmyra

Fayette

Manchester

Finger Lakes

New York

Colesville •

• South Bainbridge

Harmony

Pennsylvania

Susquehanna River

N
W ✦ E
S

this week:

WHERE ARE WE?

*D&C Section 12-17;
Joseph Smith History
1:66-75*

**Harmony, PA;
Fayette, NY**

LITTLE PICTURE

How to understand each section and apply principles to my life

- **D&C 12:**
  - **Revelation Given Through:** Joseph Smith
  - **Revelation Given To:** Joseph Knight Sr.
  - **Revelation Given When/Where:** May 1829 in Harmony, Pennsylvania
  - **Before You Read:** Joseph Knight Sr. asked Joseph Smith to ask God for this revelation. Joseph Knight Sr. had employed Joseph Smith 4 years earlier, and had since become a believer. He had been a friend of the Smith family and had given financial assistance to Joseph and Emma.
  - **What You'll Read About:** The Lord declares that the field is ready to harvest and all those who will serve are called to the work. Joseph Knight Sr. is told that when we work in God's kingdom and are humble, we will enjoy everlasting salvation.

- **D&C 13:**
  - **Revelation Given Through:** John the Baptist
  - **Revelation Given To:** Joseph Smith and Oliver Cowdery
  - **Revelation Given When/Where:** May 1829 near Harmony, Pennsylvania
  - **Before You Read:** Joseph and Oliver had read about baptism while translating the Book of Mormon. They went to the woods to pray about it and were visited by John the Baptist. This verse comes directly from Joseph's history as recorded in Joseph Smith-History 1:69.
  - **What You'll Read About:** These are the words of John the Baptist when he ordained Joseph Smith and Oliver Cowdery to the Aaronic Priesthood.

- **D&C 14:**
  - **Revelation Given Through:** Joseph Smith
  - **Revelation Given To:** David Whitmer
  - **Revelation Given When/Where:** June 1829 in Fayette, New York
  - **Before You Read:** David Whitmer had learned about Joseph from Oliver Cowdery. The Whitmer family, headed by Peter and Mary, offered Joseph and Emma free room and board in Fayette, New York while they finished the translation of the Book of Mormon. David and his brothers asked for a revelation that would clarify what role each brother should take in the work. (Sections 15 and 16 are revelations for David's brothers.)
  - **What You'll Read About:** The Lord teaches David that eternal life is the greatest gift of God, and we should stand as a witness of what we hear and see. David is called to assist in the work and promised a great reward.

- **D&C 15:**
  - **Revelation Given Through:** Joseph Smith
  - **Revelation Given To:** John Whitmer
  - **Revelation Given When/Where:** June 1829 in Fayette, New York
  - **Before You Read:** While Joseph and Emma stayed with the Whitmers, Joseph received this revelation for John Whitmer. (Sections 14 and 16 are revelations for John's brothers.)
  - **What You'll Read About:** The Lord reveals something only He and John know: John has been praying about what will be of most worth to him. The Lord teaches John that the thing of most worth will be to declare repentance to many people.

- **D&C 16:**
  - **Revelation Given Through:** Joseph Smith
  - **Revelation Given To:** Peter Whitmer Jr.
  - **Revelation Given When/Where:** June 1829 in Fayette, New York
  - **Before You Read:** While Joseph and Emma stayed with the Whitmers, Joseph received this revelation for Peter Whitmer Jr. (Sections 14 and 15 are revelations for Peter's brothers.)
  - **What You'll Read About:** The Lord gives Peter a similar revelation as he did to John in D&C 15, teaching him that the thing that is of most worth is to preach repentance to many people.

- **D&C 17:**
  - **Revelation Given Through:** Joseph Smith
  - **Revelation Given To:** Oliver Cowdery, David Whitmer, and Martin Harris
  - **Revelation Given When/Where:** June 1829 in Fayette, New York
  - **Before You Read:** The Book of Mormon says that there will be three witnesses. Oliver, David and Martin all felt inspired to be those witnesses, so Joseph asked the Lord. He received this revelation in response.
  - **What You'll Read About:** This revelation calls Oliver, David, and Martin to be the Three Witnesses to the Book of Mormon, and instructs them on their responsibilities after seeing the plates. The Lord also gives His testimony of the Book of Mormon.

- **Joseph Smith-History 1:66-75**
  - **Before You Read:** These verses cover Joseph's account of the story that takes place from around the start of D&C 6 (when we first meet Oliver Cowdery) through D&C 13 (when Joseph and Oliver receive the Aaronic priesthood and baptize one another).
  - **What You'll Read About:** Oliver Cowdery arrives in Harmony and quickly becomes Joseph's scribe for the translation of the Book of Mormon. They see a vision of John the Baptist who ordains them to the Aaronic priesthood, and instructs them on how to baptize one another. Oliver and Joseph baptize one another, and each receive the spirit of prophecy upon emerging from the water. We then get to hear Oliver's account of these "days never to be forgotten", especially focusing on his miraculous experience seeing the heavenly John the Baptist and receiving the Aaronic priesthood with Joseph Smith.

SPIRITUAL GUIDING QUESTIONS

Question: What is Joseph Knight Sr. asked to do by the Lord? How can we follow this, too?
(D&C 12:8)

Question: What specific keys does the Aaronic priesthood include? How has the Aaronic Priesthood blessed your life? How can you feel more appreciation for this Godly power?
(D&C 13:1)

Question: What is considered the greatest gift that God can give? What are you willing to do in order to receive this gift? (D&C 14:7)

Question: Why is preaching repentance such a worthwhile goal in life? (D&C 16:6)

Question: What is the role of faith in seeing these items? Why do you think these men needed to have faith in order to see them? (D&C 17:2-3)

Question: What were they commanded to do after they had seen the plates and other items? Why do you think this part was important? (D&C 17:5)

Question: What blessings and gifts did Joseph and Oliver receive after being baptized? What does that teach about the power of baptism? (JS-H 1:73-74)

ADDITIONAL THOUGHTS AND NOTES

D&C 18

"The Worth of Souls Is Great"

BIG PICTURE

How to feel confident fitting in this week's readings with the entire Doctrine & Covenants

General Context:

- **The section we are studying this week marks a new focus: Organizing a church.** Up until this point, many of the revelations and directions from the Lord had been focused on the coming forth of the Book of Mormon. Joseph's entire purpose was centered on translating this ancient record.

- **But now, the Book of Mormon translation was almost complete.** Joseph, Emma, and Oliver Cowdery were living at the Whitmer family farm in Fayette, New York. Oliver Cowdery, David Whitmer, and Martin Harris had been selected as the Three Witnesses and been allowed to see the gold plates along with a spiritual manifestation. It was the summer of 1829.

- **If we spoil the story a bit and look ahead a few months, it was April of 1830 when the Church of Jesus Christ of Latter-day Saints was officially organized in this dispensation.** So this summer before was starting to fill with revelations about the actual structure that the restored Church should have, and what their priorities should be.

- **You'll notice in D&C 18 that the Lord gives specific direction about the Quorum of the Twelve Apostles.** After receiving this revelation, Oliver and David spent the next few years searching for the 12 men who would comprise this quorum. This quorum was not officially organized until 1835 in Kirtland, Ohio.

Spiritual Themes:

Look for these themes as you read this week! Find examples in the scriptures, and ponder on what these themes can look like in your life.

- **The Church and the Gospel of Christ**

- **The Worth of Souls**

- **The Roles of the Twelve Apostles**

People to Know:

- **Oliver Cowdery**
  - Oliver Cowdery was a young school teacher who briefly lived at the Smith family home in Manchester. In April 1829, he became Joseph's new scribe for the Book of Mormon translation process. Oliver and Joseph received many revelations together. These two also received the Aaronic priesthood from John the Baptist on May 15, 1829. Joseph and Oliver baptized each other.
  - Following growing persecution, Oliver went with Joseph and Emma to live at the Whitmer farm in Fayette, New York. Oliver was good friends with David Whitmer. Oliver assisted in the completion of the translation of the Book of Mormon there, and was one of the official Three Witnesses of the gold plates.
  - Oliver played a huge role in officially organizing the Church. He asked Joseph questions about it as early as June 1829, and received a revelation calling him to repentance and instructing him on how to proceed.
- **David Whitmer**
  - David lived in Fayette, New York with his parents, Peter and Mary, and many siblings. David became good friends with Oliver Cowdery when Oliver was teaching in Manchester. When Oliver wrote to David, asking if his family could host Joseph, Emma, and Oliver as they finished the translation, David helped make that happen. David asked Joseph for a revelation once he was residing in their home in June 1829, and Joseph received one for him.
  - David was moved with a righteous desire to be one of the Three Witnesses of the Book of Mormon, and was officially called to be one of them, seeing the plates in June 1829. David was also given a revelation, along with Oliver, to repent because the worth of souls is great as they prepared to organize a Church.
- **Joseph Smith**
  - Joseph, now safely housed at the Whitmer farm in Fayette, was finishing up the translation process for the Book of Mormon. He had received revelations on behalf of many individuals who were seeking to know the will of God in their lives.
  - Joseph confirmed with God that Oliver Cowdery, Martin Harris, and David Whitmer were to be the Three Witnesses. There were also 8 other Whitmer and Smith family members who served as Eight Witnesses to the gold plates.
  - Joseph was now starting to receive more revelation about the organization of a Church that would bring the restored gospel of Jesus Christ to the world.

Where are We?

- **Fayette, NY**
  - This is where the Whitmer family lived. Peter Whitmer Sr. owned a farm here, and many of his children lived with them. His son, David, became good friends with Oliver Cowdery. Oliver asked the Whitmer family if he, Joseph, and Emma could move to their home while they finished the Book of Mormon translation, due to growing opposition in Harmony.
  - The Book of Mormon translation was completed here at the Whitmer home in the summer of 1829, and Joseph received revelations for three of the Whitmer sons.
  - It was here that Oliver, Martin, and David became the Three Witnesses to the Book of Mormon, and learned about the future organization of the Church.

Fayette
New York

←Palmyra

←Manchester

New York

Whitmer
Home and Farm

Cayuga
Lake

● Fayette
Township

Seneca
Lake

this week:

WHERE ARE WE?

D&C Section 18
Fayette, NY

Keuka
Lake

N
W—◇—E
S

Finger Lakes

LITTLE PICTURE

How to understand each section and apply principles to my life

- **D&C 18:**
  - **Revelation Given Through:** Joseph Smith
  - **Revelation Given To:** Joseph Smith, Oliver Cowdery, and David Whitmer
  - **Revelation Given When/Where:** June 1829 in Fayette, New York
  - **Before You Read:** This section includes instructions given to Joseph Smith, Oliver Cowdery, and David Whitmer, apparently in response to a question Oliver asked the Lord.
  - **What You'll Read About:** Oliver Cowdery is told that the Church will be organized after the pattern in the Book of Mormon. Oliver and David are told to repent because the worth of souls is great in the sight of God. They are told to preach repentance, and invite others to be baptized in Christ's name. They are also asked to start seeking out who will be the first twelve apostles. The Lord teaches some of the roles the apostles will take on.

SPIRITUAL GUIDING QUESTIONS

Question: How do the gospel of Jesus Christ and the Church work together? How can we ensure that the Church will not fail? (D&C 18:4-5)

Question: How does knowing that the worth of souls is great in the sight of God affect your view of the world, yourself, and those you live around? (D&C 18:10)

Question: Why do you think we feel great joy when we bring people unto the Savior? Have you felt that joy before? (D&C 18:15-16)

Question: What does it mean to you that you can do nothing without faith, hope, and charity? (D&C 18:19)

Question: Have you ever been proud to be given someone's name or title? How do you feel when you take Jesus Christ's name upon yourself? What does this look like? (D&C 18:22-24)

Question: How are Oliver and David supposed to search out the Twelve? What kind of people are they looking for? (D&C 18:26-29, 37-38)

Question: How have members of the current Quorum of the Twelve Apostles been a blessing in your life? (D&C 18:27-28)

ADDITIONAL THOUGHTS AND NOTES

D&C 19

"Learn of Me"

BIG PICTURE

How to feel confident fitting in this week's readings with the entire Doctrine & Covenants

General Context:

- **The focus of this week is the printing of the Book of Mormon and the role that Martin Harris played in it.** Martin Harris had an interesting relationship with Joseph Smith so far. He was much older than Joseph, much more successful, and his farm that he had established meant that he had much more money. Martin had willingly helped Joseph and Emma financially when they needed to move from Manchester to Harmony shortly after receiving the gold plates. And Martin scribed for Joseph for many months in early 1828 in Harmony. But Martin's wife, Lucy Harris, was concerned about her husband's choice to continually financially and emotionally support Joseph– especially when he had refused to show her the gold plates. This is what led to Martin repeatedly asking Joseph for permission to take some of the manuscript pages to his wife, where they were ultimately lost.

- **Now, almost a year after the lost manuscript pages incident, Martin was being asked to contribute to the Restoration in a dramatic way.** It was the summer of 1829, and Joseph had completely finished translating the Book of Mormon. It was ready to be published, but it was going to take $3,000 to print 5,000 copies. Martin Harris was the only person Joseph knew with enough money to be able to finance this. This was a large amount of money, even for Martin, and he knew that his wife would not want him to mortgage the family farm to print a book she didn't believe in.

- **This is when Joseph received the revelation known as D&C 19 directing Martin Harris to finance the printing of the book.** Martin mortgaged his family farm and obeyed the commandment. The Book of Mormon was finally printed and ready to share with the world! It's interesting to note that about a year later, after sales for the Book of Mormon were low, Martin followed the commandment in verse 35 of this Section to actually sell enough of his property to pay the debt to the printer.

- **But there's something else extremely important in this revelation this week: We get the only firsthand account of the Savior Himself describing what it was like to atone for the sins of all mankind.** In the New Testament, we get narration from other people about Jesus Christ's experience in the Garden of Gethsemane and on the cross at Calvary. But in D&C 19, the Lord is speaking directly to Martin and talks about sacrifice and suffering. Verses 16-19 give us a humbling and unique perspective for what Jesus Christ experienced.

Spiritual Themes:

Look for these themes as you read this week! Find examples in the scriptures, and ponder on what these themes can look like in your life.

- **The Gift of Repentance**

- **Christ's Suffering on Our Behalf**

- **Sacrificing for God's Kingdom**

People to Know:

- **Martin Harris**
  - Martin was older and wealthier than Joseph. They became good friends while Joseph was waiting for the gold plates. When Joseph needed to move to Harmony, Pennsylvania with his wife to escape the persecution and those trying to steal the plates, Martin gave him $50 as a gift to help get him there.
  - Martin took a copy of some of the characters to scholars in New York, and got confirmation that the characters were reformed Egyptian. Martin followed Joseph to Harmony, and took over for Emma as Joseph's scribe. Martin's wife, Lucy, also stayed with them for a bit, but was skeptical that Joseph never showed anyone the plates.
  - Martin wanted to show his wife some of the transcriptions so that she would be pleased that he was investing money in the church, and asked Joseph for some of the manuscript pages. After being given some, he lost them, and felt great remorse when he had to tell Joseph.
  - After staying in Palmyra for a while, Martin visited Joseph in Harmony to see how Joseph was doing. He was delighted that Joseph had been forgiven by the Lord and was preparing to start translating again. Joseph received a revelation in March 1829 that tells Martin to believe Joseph's testimony, and that Martin can be a witness to the Book of Mormon at some point.
  - A few months later, and with a strong desire to be one of the Three Witnesses, he was called to be one, along with Oliver Cowdery and David Whitmer. Although Martin originally felt he wasn't worthy to see the plates, he became a witness in June 1829.
  - Joseph was ready to publish the Book of Mormon, although he would need a lot of money for any publisher to agree. Joseph Smith received a revelation where the Lord called Martin to repentance, and asked him to finance the printing of the Book of Mormon and pay off other debts. In the summer of 1829, Martin did this, and the Book of Mormon was printed!

Where are We?

- **Manchester, NY**
    - This is where the Smith family lived.
    - Joseph and Emma moved away from here after neighbors started becoming hostile, but the Smith family continued to reside here, giving Joseph a place to stay whenever he needed to come back home.
    - Oliver Cowdery, a local school teacher, stayed here at the Smith home, which is where he learned about Joseph before offering to be Joseph's scribe.
    - After the Book of Mormon was completely translated, the Eight Witnesses saw the gold plates in the woods by the Smith farm.

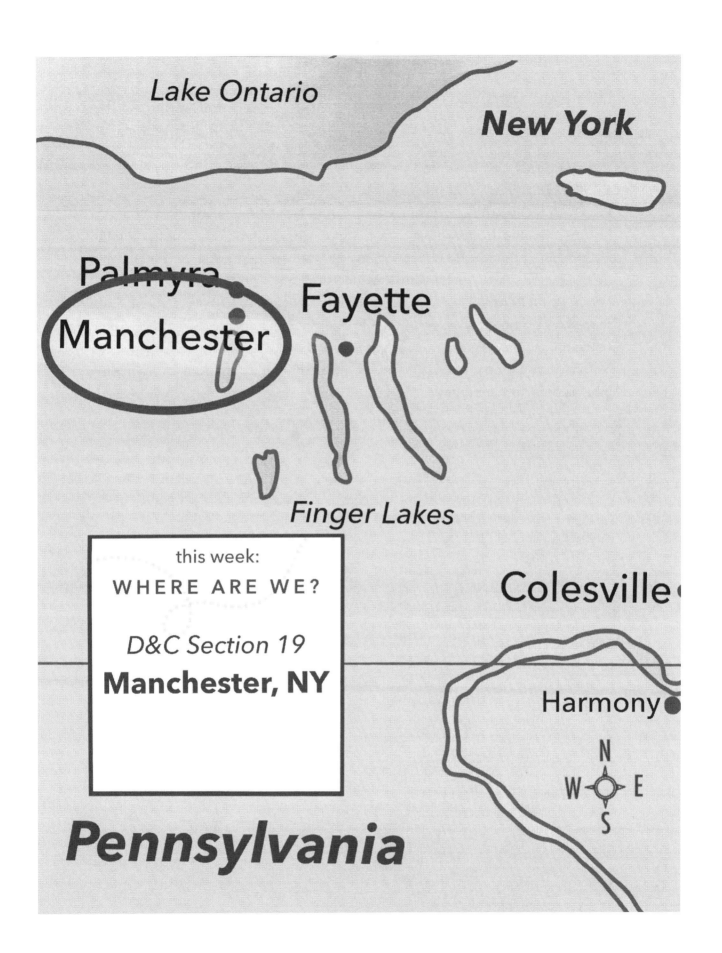

Lake Ontario

New York

Palmyra

Manchester

Fayette

Finger Lakes

this week:
WHERE ARE WE?

D&C Section 19
Manchester, NY

Colesville

Harmony

N
W E
S

Pennsylvania

LITTLE PICTURE

How to understand each section and apply principles to my life

- **D&C 19:**
    - **Revelation Given Through:** Joseph Smith
    - **Revelation Given To:** Martin Harris
    - **Revelation Given When/Where:** Summer 1829 in Manchester, New York
    - **Before You Read:** Joseph Smith and Martin Harris were in negotiations with Egbert B. Grandin of Palmyra to print the Book of Mormon. No one among the early believers had the financial assets to fund the printing other than Martin Harris.
    - **What You'll Read About:** All must all repent or face God's punishment. The Savior then shares a firsthand experience of His atoning sacrifice. The Lord gives various commandments including to learn of Him, not covet, and preach repentance. Finally, Martin is commanded to finance the printing of the Book of Mormon and to pay his debt to the printer.

SPIRITUAL GUIDING QUESTIONS

Question: Why is it essential that we repent? What happens if we do? What happens if we do not? (D&C 19:4-12)

Question: What emotions do you feel as you read about the Savior's account of His atoning sacrifice? How do your emotions while reading this encourage you to want to change? (D&C 19:16-19)

Question: How do you feel peace in Christ? (D&C 19:23)

Question: What are some circumstances where you feel tempted to covet? How can you get rid of those feelings and turn more to the Lord? (D&C 19:25-26)

Question: What is one way you could more publicly declare your faith? Why is it important to share what we believe? (D&C 19:29-30)

Question: What does the Lord's counsel to Martin Harris teach us about our priorities in life? What sacrifices have you made for your faith? (D&C 19:33-36)

Question: What stands out to you as you read the final three questions in the final three verses? (D&C 19:39-41)

ADDITIONAL THOUGHTS AND NOTES

D&C 20 - 22

"The Rise of the Church of Christ"

BIG PICTURE

How to feel confident fitting in this week's readings with the entire Doctrine & Covenants

General Context:

- **These three sections cover the official organization of the Church of Christ.** All of the sections were given in April of 1830, with the first two happening in Fayette at the Whitmer farm, and the last one occurring in Manchester, where Joseph Smith Sr.'s family lived. We will study:
  - **D&C 20** (a longer section!) which was originally called the "Articles and Covenants" of the Church. Think of this as the first general handbook, as it lays out important duties and direction for the brand new Church. This revelation was received BEFORE the Church's organization.
  - **D&C 21** declares that Joseph Smith is officially called as a prophet, seer, translator, and apostle of Jesus Christ. This revelation was received DURING the Church's organization.
  - **D&C 22** clarifies that even if people had been previously baptized by other churches, they need to be rebaptized by proper priesthood authority into the Church of Christ. This revelation was received shortly AFTER the Church's organization.
- **Why did Joseph choose April 6, 1830 to organize the Church?** Well, Joseph didn't choose the date at all! As we can see in both D&C 20 and D&C 21, the Lord Himself told Joseph Smith to organize the Church on April 6, 1830. People close to Joseph knew starting in the summer of 1830 (which was when the last revelation we studied occurred) that both he and Oliver had mentioned that they were working towards organizing a Church. However, no one knew exact details of when or where this would happen.
- **Finally, on April 6, 1830 in the Whitmer home, the Church was officially organized.** There were 30 or 40 people, men and women, in attendance. 6 people, including Joseph and Oliver, were recognized as the founding members of the Church. At this meeting, they had an opening prayer, Joseph and Oliver ordained each other as elders, they all partook of the sacrament, Joseph and Oliver gave the gift of the Holy Ghost to those who had been baptized, and Joseph received the revelation known as D&C 21.

Spiritual Themes:

Look for these themes as you read this week! Find examples in the scriptures, and ponder on what these themes can look like in your life.

- **The Importance of Church Organization**

- **Following the Prophet**

- **Proper Authority in Baptism**

People to Know:

- **Oliver Cowdery**
    - Oliver was a school teacher who boarded with the Smith family for a short time. It was here that Joseph Smith Sr. and Lucy Smith taught Oliver about their son and his visions. Oliver was immediately interested.
    - Oliver traveled to Harmony, Pennsylvania to meet Joseph Smith. Oliver ended up becoming a scribe for the prophet and the two men received the Aaronic priesthood from John the Baptist.
    - Oliver helped Joseph and Emma move to Fayette to the Whitmer farm in order to escape persecution. Oliver helped Joseph finish up the translation of the Book of Mormon, and he was able to be one of the Three Witnesses.
    - Oliver started asking questions about what the Church should be like, and it is many of his questions that prompted Joseph Smith to ask and receive revelations that detailed the beginning of the Church of Christ.
    - When the Church was officially organized on April 6, 1830, Oliver Cowdery was chosen as the second elder of the Church.
- **Joseph Smith**
    - Joseph had finished translating the entire Book of Mormon at the Whitmer farm in Fayette, New York. He had worked with Martin Harris to get the book published.
    - Joseph spent the summer and end of 1829 with Oliver, asking many questions to the Lord about how to organize the Church that would bring His gospel to the world.
    - On the date revealed by the Lord Himself, Joseph Smith organized the Church of Christ on April 6, 1830 at the Whitmer farm. Joseph was recognized as the first elder of the Church.

Where are We?

- **Fayette, NY**
  - This is where the Whitmer family lived. The Book of Mormon translation was completed here at the Whitmer home in the summer of 1829, and Joseph received revelations for three of the Whitmer sons.
  - It was here that Oliver, Martin, and David became the Three Witnesses to the Book of Mormon, and learned about the future organization of the Church.
  - On April 6, 1830, the "Church of Christ" was officially organized here in the Whitmer home. Joseph and Oliver ordained each other, and over 40 women and men were in attendance.
- **Manchester, NY**
  - This is where the Smith family lived. Joseph and Emma moved away from this home after neighbors started becoming hostile, but the Smith family continued to reside here, giving Joseph a place to stay whenever he needed to come back home.
  - After the Book of Mormon was completely translated, the Eight Witnesses saw the gold plates in the woods by the Smith farm.
  - Right after the official organization of the Church in April 1830, Joseph came to Manchester a few times and received various revelations about baptism and mission calls.

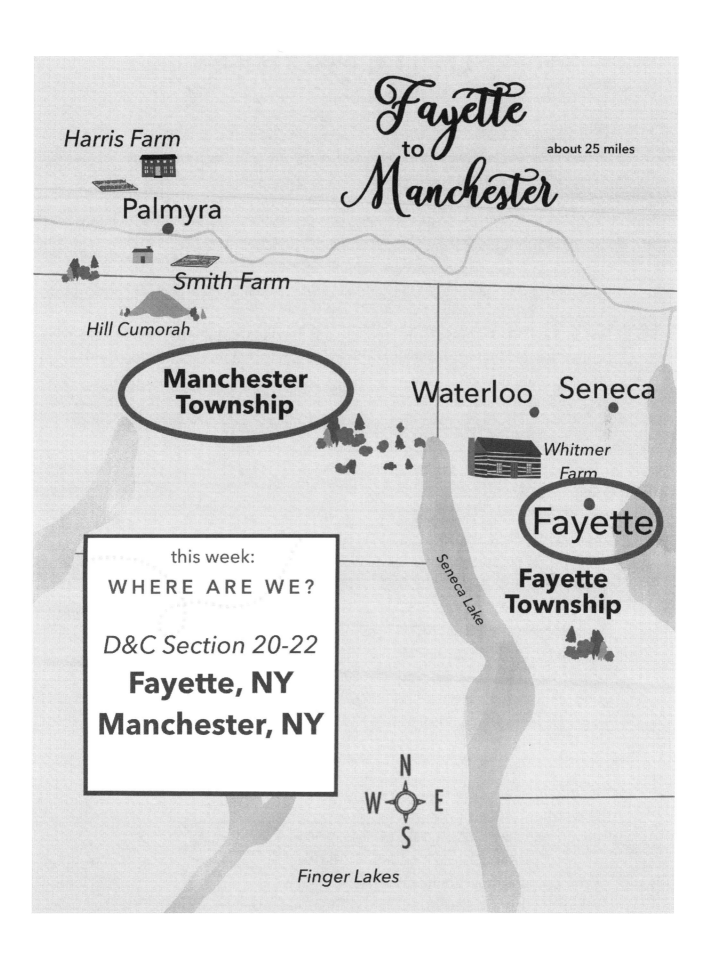

Fayette to Manchester

about 25 miles

Harris Farm

Palmyra

Smith Farm

Hill Cumorah

Manchester Township

Waterloo

Seneca

Whitmer Farm

Fayette

Fayette Township

Seneca Lake

this week:

WHERE ARE WE?

D&C Section 20-22
Fayette, NY
Manchester, NY

N
W E
S

Finger Lakes

LITTLE PICTURE

How to understand each section and apply principles to my life

- **D&C 20:**
  - **Revelation Given Through:** Joseph Smith
  - **Revelation Given To:** The Church
  - **Revelation Given When/Where:** April 1830 in Fayette, New York
  - **Before You Read:** As Joseph and Oliver were working towards the organization of the Church, they had many questions. This section was received at some point leading up to the organization of the Church on April 6, 1830, and is called the "Articles and Covenants" of the Church. It was essentially the general handbook of instructions at the time!
  - **What You'll Read About:** The Lord lays out the origins of the Church, including the call of Joseph Smith and coming forth of the Book of Mormon. The elders of the Church share their testimony of God and Christ. The basic doctrines and beliefs of the Church are laid out. The section then includes instructions for baptism and the duties of various priesthood offices. Instructions are given for administering the sacrament and keeping track of membership.

- **D&C 21:**
  - **Revelation Given Through:** Joseph Smith
  - **Revelation Given To:** The Church
  - **Revelation Given When/Where:** April 1830 in Fayette, New York
  - **Before You Read:** This revelation was received during the organization of the Church on April 6, 1830. The meeting took place in Peter Whitmer Sr.'s home, and included the participation of six men, ordination of Joseph Smith and Oliver Cowdery, and the administration of the sacrament.
  - **What You'll Read About:** The Lord declares that Joseph Smith is called as a seer and prophet, and calls on the Church to listen to his commandments. The Lord will bless all who labor in His vineyard.

- **D&C 22:**
  - **Revelation Given Through:** Joseph Smith
  - **Revelation Given To:** The Church
  - **Revelation Given When/Where:** April 1830 in Manchester, New York
  - **Before You Read:** Some believers wondered if they needed to be re-baptized if they had previously been baptized in other churches.
  - **What You'll Read About:** The Lord clarifies that even if someone has been baptized in another church, they must be re-baptized by proper authority into this Church. Baptism by proper authority is the gate through which we must pass.

SPIRITUAL GUIDING QUESTIONS

Question: Where do you see evidence that God is the same yesterday, today, and forever? How does that bring you peace? (D&C 20:12)

Question: Why is it important to be reminded of doctrinal truths often? (D&C 20:17-36)

Question: What are the duties of each office of the Priesthood? Whether or not you hold that office, how can you help fulfill those duties within the church? (D&C 20:38-67)

Question: What titles are Joseph called to? How do these titles differentiate from each other? (D&C 21:1)

Question: What specific blessings are we promised if we listen to the prophets? Have you seen evidence of these in your life? (D&C 21:6)

Question: Which covenants did you make at baptism? How do those affect your life today? (D&C 22:1-2)

Question: Why does proper authority matter when it comes to ordinances? (D&C 22:2)

ADDITIONAL THOUGHTS AND NOTES

D&C 23 - 26

"Seek for the Things of a Better World"

BIG PICTURE

How to feel confident fitting in this week's readings with the entire Doctrine & Covenants

General Context:

- **The young, newly established Church was experiencing a lot of opposition right off the bat.** It is in contrast with these great trials that the revelations we are studying this week were given. You'll remember that the Church was organized in April 1830 in Fayette, New York, after which Joseph had gone to Manchester to his parents' home for a bit. This week, we will read:
    - **D&C 23** (April 1830 in Manchester) where Joseph received revelation for 5 men who had requested it.
    - **D&C 24, 25, and 26** (July 1830 in Harmony) are revelations received AFTER experiencing great trials in June and July. D&C 24 is for Joseph and Oliver, D&C 25 is for Emma, and D&C 26 is teaching Joseph, Oliver, and John Whitmer about the law of common consent.

- **What were some of these big trials occurring in June and July 1830?** To put it simply, the people living in that area of New York did not like that a new Church was being established, nor did they like that Joseph was preaching. This dislike turned into mobs of violence. In fact, in June, Emma Smith and many others were ready to be baptized and officially join the Church. They were in Colesville, New York, which is where Joseph Knight Sr., a friend of Joseph Smith, lived. A mob tried to prevent the baptisms from happening in the first place, and they gathered to yell, mock, and disturb the baptisms when they actually took place. They later surrounded the Knight home in Colesville where the newly baptized members were planning to receive the gift of the Holy Ghost. Joseph Smith ended up being arrested, released, and arrested again, tired, acquitted, and threatened by mobs who wanted to tar and feather him. After Joseph was released, he and Emma went back to Harmony to grapple with everything that had just occurred and find some rest.

- **What is the importance of Colesville?** Joseph Knight Sr.'s family was the anchor of the Church in Colesville, and Colesville is often considered the first official congregation of the Church. Many Colesville saints endured the hectic and threatening baptismal experience with Emma, and they still were waiting for Joseph and Oliver to give them the gift of the Holy Ghost, since a mob had interrupted their plans. These Colesville saints became known for their amazing faith. We will learn more about them in future sections!

- **What does D&C 25 teach us about Emma?** The revelation in D&C 25 is unique because it is the only official revelation that was received directly for Emma. Think about what she had endured up to that point in her life. She had married Joseph, helped scribe for him, and then lost their first baby in Harmony. She had mourned with her husband during some dark times and then moved to Fayette for the completion of the translation process and the organization of the Church. When she was ready to be baptized, she endured a chaotic and threatening experience along with the Colesville saints, after which her husband was arrested. She gathered with other women to pray for her husband's safety. When he finally was released, they went back to Harmony, near Emma's family, to recuperate. Emma was now 26 years old and needed to know that God knew her, and that she had a role to fulfill.
- **What is the law of common consent?** D&C 26 mentions that Joseph and the other Church leaders should use the law of common consent in everything they do. In fact, you might remember in D&C 21, on the day the Church was officially organized, the members unanimously sustained Joseph Smith as the prophet, seer, and apostle. This is the same exact system we use for callings and priesthood ordinations today. Common consent means that everyone generally agrees with a calling or ordination, and that each person is willing to sustain, pray for, and assist that person in their duties. **Common consent does NOT mean 2 things, though:**
  - Common consent DOESN'T mean that we have "majority rules" where we take sides and vote.
  - Common consent DOESN'T mean that everyone always agrees. There are many instances throughout Church history and still today where someone disagrees with a new calling or ordination. If this is the case, the issues are not handled publicly, like in a debate, but instead are handled privately. This could lead to a new name being put forth for a calling.

Spiritual Themes:

Look for these themes as you read this week! Find examples in the scriptures, and ponder on what these themes can look like in your life.

- **Patience in Afflictions**

- **Humility and Aligning Our Will with God's**

- **Power of Sacred Hymns**

People to Know:

- **Oliver Cowdery**
    - Oliver Cowdery started off as a young school teacher who lived at the Smith family home in Manchester. He learned about Joseph's visions and ultimately traveled to Harmony to become Joseph's new scribe. Oliver was with Joseph when they received the Aaronic priesthood from John the Baptist.
    - Oliver arranged their move to Fayette to the Whitmer home in order to escape persecution. At the Whitmer home, Joseph and Oliver finished the translation of the Book of Mormon and officially organized the Church. Oliver was named as the second elder of the Church and was one of the Three Witnesses of the gold plates.
    - He went with Joseph and Emma to Harmony to escape persecution yet again in the summer of 1830, where Oliver was given more counsel about his duties in the Church.
- **Hyrum Smith**
    - Hyrum was Joseph's older brother. Hyrum had already received revelation through Joseph that he should prepare to serve a mission. Hyrum was one of the Eight Witnesses to the Book of Mormon, along with his brother Samuel and his father.
    - After the Book of Mormon was published and the Church was organized, Hyrum asked Joseph what his duties should be in the new Church. In April 1830, along with 4 other brethren, Hyrum was given a revelation that he is under no condemnation. He was also specifically counseled that his heart and tongue are ready to preach and strengthen the Church.
- **Samuel H. Smith**
    - Samuel was the younger brother of the prophet Joseph. Samuel was the one who accompanied his teacher, Oliver Cowdery, to go visit Joseph and Emma in Harmony.
    - Later, Samuel went to visit his brother again, and Joseph preached the gospel to him. Samuel went into the woods alone, and came back with a firm witness that what his brother had taught him was true. He was baptized by Oliver Cowdery and became one of the first traveling missionaries in the church.
    - After the Book of Mormon was published and the Church was organized, Samuel, along with 4 other brethren, asked Joseph what his duties should be in the new Church in April 1830. Samuel was given revelation that he was under no condemnation, and that he should strengthen the Church.

- **Joseph Smith Sr.**
  - A very supportive father to Joseph, he was the first person that Joseph told about many of the visions he experienced while growing up. He supported Joseph in keeping the plates hidden after he had obtained them.
  - After the fiasco with Martin Harris and the lost manuscript pages, Joseph Sr. was concerned about his son's well-being. He knew Joseph Jr. had lost the ability to translate for a while, and was concerned that he wasn't hearing from him as often. He went to visit Joseph Jr. in Harmony, Pennsylvania.
  - While Joseph Sr. was in Harmony, discovering that his son was doing fine again, Joseph Jr. received a revelation for his father. This revelation in February 1829 spoke about Joseph Sr.'s desires and his qualification to do missionary work.
  - Back at his home in Palmyra, New York, Joseph Sr. and his family hosted the local teacher, Oliver Cowdery, in their home. Oliver asked Joseph Sr. many questions about his son and his visions and plates. Joseph Sr. eventually opened up and that is what led Oliver to believe that he was called to assist Joseph in his work of translation.
  - In June 1829, Joseph Sr. was able to be one of the Eight Witnesses of the Book of Mormon, along with his sons Hyrum and Samuel.
  - After the Book of Mormon was published and the Church of Christ was formed, Joseph Sr. wanted to know what his duties in the new Church would be. Joseph Jr. received a revelation for him and 4 other men who asked the same question. Joseph Sr. was told that he was under no condemnation and that he should strengthen the Church. Shortly thereafter, he was baptized into the Church.
- **Joseph Knight Sr.**
  - Joseph Knight Sr. hired Joseph Smith to work on his farm, and ultimately became a great friend to the Smith family. He was even present when Joseph arrived home after obtaining the gold plates. The Knight family lived in Colesville, New York.
  - Joseph Knight sent some supplies and money to Joseph and Emma while they were translating the plates in Harmony. Joseph received a revelation for Joseph Knight in May 1829.
  - After the Book of Mormon had been published and the Church had been organized, Joseph Knight asked Joseph what his duties should be in the new Church, along with 4 other brethren. In April 1830, Joseph Smith received a revelation that Joseph Knight needed to pray vocally and in secret, and that he should be baptized while using his words to preach. Joseph and his wife, Polly, were later baptized and confirmed members of the Church, despite great opposition in Colesville where they resided.

- **Emma Hale Smith**
  - Emma met Joseph when he was hired to work near her family farm in Harmony, Pennsylvania. Her parents did not initially like Joseph, but Emma and Joseph eventually got married and moved in with his parents in Manchester, New York in January of 1827.
  - Emma was the first scribe for Joseph's translation of the Book of Mormon. The pair moved back to Harmony to live by her parents and continue the translation during Emma's pregnancy. Martin Harris took over most of the scribe duties at that point. Tragically, Emma lost their first baby.
  - After Oliver had moved in with Emma and Joseph and taken over as scribe, the three moved to Fayette to be with the Whitmer family, where Emma scribed some more for Joseph.
  - Emma was baptized along with the saints in Colesville (including the Knight family), but intense persecution drove them away before she could be confirmed. Joseph was also receiving revelation that he shouldn't worry about material things and should focus on his ministry. In the face of her worries and concern, Joseph received a revelation in July 1830 that reminded her that she was blessed and an "elect lady". She was given greater perspective and asked to support her husband, in addition to being asked to create a hymnal.
- **John Whitmer**
  - John was David Whitmer's brother, a son of Peter and Mary. Joseph stayed at John's father's residence in Fayette, New York to finish the translation of the Book of Mormon.
  - John asked Joseph for a revelation while Joseph was at their home translating in June of 1829, and was given what is considered to be one of the most personal revelations, revealing that the Lord knew he had been asking for what would be the most worthwhile thing to do.
  - John was one of the Eight Witnesses of the Book of Mormon, along with his brothers Christian, Jacob, and Peter Jr, and his brother-in-law Hiram Page. This witness occurred at the Smith family farm in Manchester shortly after the Three Witnesses saw the plates in Fayette.

Where are We?

- **Manchester, NY**
  - This is where the Smith family lived.
  - After the Book of Mormon was completely translated, the Eight Witnesses saw the gold plates in the woods by the Smith farm.
  - Right after the official organization of the Church in April 1830, Joseph came to Manchester a few times and received various revelations about baptism and mission calls.
- **Harmony, Pennsylvania**
  - Emma Hale Smith's family lived in Harmony.
  - Emma scribed for Joseph here in Harmony until Martin Harris showed up and took over. Oliver Cowdery later joined the group here and became the new scribe. The Aaronic priesthood was restored in the nearby woods. After persecution in Harmony started to grow, Joseph, Emma, and Oliver moved to Fayette to finish translating the Book of Mormon. They kept their home and farm in Harmony, returning from time to time throughout 1830 to tend to the farm, and take care of other business.
  - By July 1830 though, it was revealed that Joseph should focus all his time and efforts on building up the Church. The Lord gave Emma a special revelation in her time of uncertainty here in Harmony prior to their final departure.

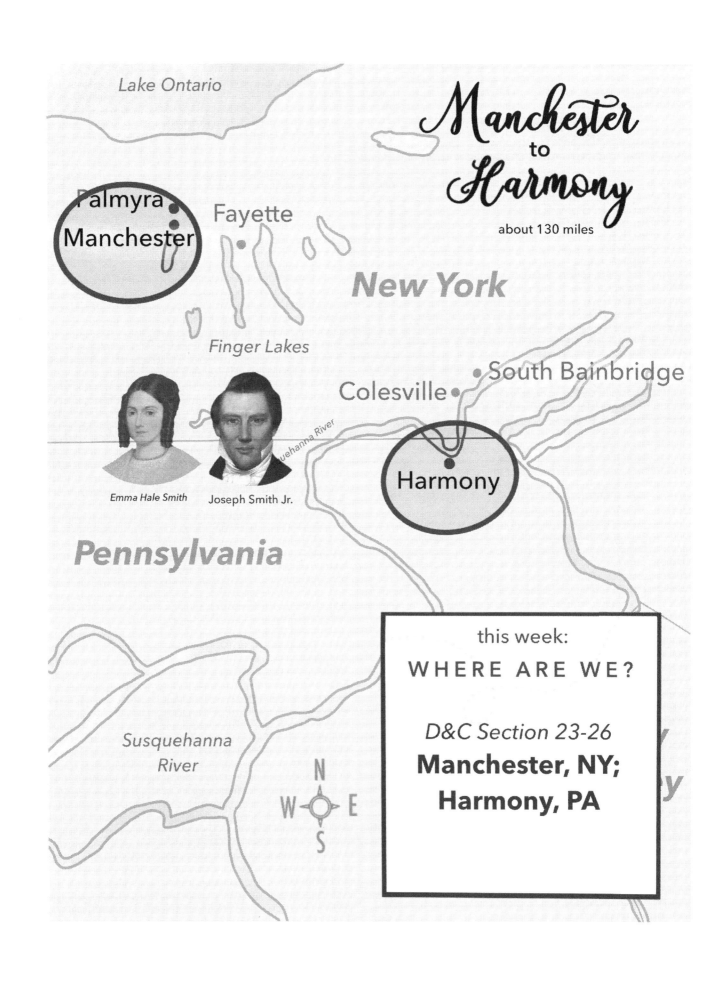

Lake Ontario

Manchester
to
Harmony

about 130 miles

Palmyra
Manchester

Fayette

New York

Finger Lakes

Colesville

South Bainbridge

Emma Hale Smith   Joseph Smith Jr.

Susquehanna River

Harmony

Pennsylvania

Susquehanna
River

N
W · E
S

this week:

WHERE ARE WE?

D&C Section 23-26
**Manchester, NY;
Harmony, PA**

LITTLE PICTURE

How to understand each section and apply principles to my life

- **D&C 23:**
  - **Revelation Given Through:** Joseph Smith
  - **Revelation Given To:** Oliver Cowdery, Hyrum Smith, Samuel H. Smith, Joseph Smith Sr., and Joseph Knight Sr.
  - **Revelation Given When/Where:** April 1830 in Manchester, New York
  - **Before You Read:** Oliver Cowdery, Hyrum Smith, Samuel H. Smith, Joseph Smith Sr., and Joseph Knight Sr. all asked Joseph Smith what their duties should be in the new Church. Joseph Smith inquired of the Lord, and these are all short responses with specific advice to each of the five men.
  - **What You'll Read About:** Oliver, Hyrum, Samuel, and Joseph Sr. are told they are under no condemnation. Joseph Knight is counseled to pray vocally and unite with the Church.

- **D&C 24:**
  - **Revelation Given Through:** Joseph Smith
  - **Revelation Given To:** Joseph Smith and Oliver Cowdery
  - **Revelation Given When/Where:** July 1830 in Harmony, Pennsylvania
  - **Before You Read:** This is a revelation given to Joseph Smith and Oliver Cowdery during a time of great persecution of the young church. Sections 24, 25 and 26 were received at the same time.
  - **What You'll Read About:** Joseph is told to magnify his office, and to go to the saints in Colesville, Fayette, and Manchester for support. He is counseled to be patient in his afflictions. Oliver is told to glory in the Lord and preach the gospel day and night. Those who preach the gospel will be protected and led by the Lord in all things.

- **D&C 25:**
  - **Revelation Given Through:** Joseph Smith
  - **Revelation Given To:** Emma Smith
  - **Revelation Given When/Where:** July 1830 in Harmony, Pennsylvania
  - **Before You Read:** This is a revelation given to Emma Smith. It was received at the same time as sections 24 and 26.
  - **What You'll Read About:** Emma is called to expound scriptures, exhort the Church, support her husband in his calling, and to receive support from him. She is also called to make a selection of hymns. The Lord tells her to rejoice and cleave to her covenants.

- **D&C 26:**
  - **Revelation Given Through:** Joseph Smith
  - **Revelation Given To:** Joseph Smith, Oliver Cowdery and John Whitmer
  - **Revelation Given When/Where:** July 1830 in Harmony, Pennsylvania
  - **Before You Read:** This is a revelation given to Joseph Smith, Oliver Cowdery and John Whitmer during a time of great persecution of the young Church. This section was received with sections 24 and 25.
  - **What You'll Read About:** Joseph, Oliver, and John are told to study the scriptures, and are taught about the law of common consent.

SPIRITUAL GUIDING QUESTIONS

Question: What specific counsel do you think the Lord would give you right now? Have you tried asking recently? (D&C 23:1-7)

Question: Have you experienced moments where words were given to you in the very moment you needed them? How do you think you can cultivate more of those moments? (D&C 24:6)

Question: The Lord says about Oliver, "I am with him to the end." If you substitute your name in there, how do you feel? How does this make you want to act? (D&C 24:10)

Question: How was Emma asked to support her husband, and how was he asked to support her? How could you better support your spouse or a loved one? (D&C 25:5-9)

Question: Does your soul delight in hymns? Which hymns have touched your heart? (D&C 25:12)

Question: How have you learned to study the scriptures, and how has it blessed your life? (D&C 26:1)

Question: What does the "law of common consent" look like in your interactions with others in the church or your family? How can you encourage this even more? (D&C 26:2)

ADDITIONAL THOUGHTS AND NOTES

D&C 27 - 28

"All Things Must Be Done in Order"

BIG PICTURE

How to feel confident fitting in this week's readings with the entire Doctrine & Covenants

General Context:

- **The Church, only a few months old at this time, still needed a lot of direction to figure out how everything should be done.** This fine-tuning and clarification will be the focus for our readings this week. We will study:
  - **D&C 27** (August 1830) is a revelation Joseph received from an angel while trying to prepare the sacrament clarifying what should and shouldn't be used in that ordinance.
  - **D&C 28** (September 1830) is a revelation telling Oliver Cowdery to serve a mission, and also clarifying that Joseph is the only one to receive revelation for the entire Church.
- **You'll remember that Emma had been part of a group of members who had been baptized in Colesville, New York in June 1830.** But their confirmations were interrupted by violent mobs and Joseph Smith's arrest. Among this group was a woman named Polly Knight. Polly and her husband Newel traveled to Harmony to visit Joseph and Emma, now 2 months following Emma and Polly's baptisms. Emma and Polly were finally able to be confirmed as members of the Church and given the gift of the Holy Ghost. As part of this sacred celebration, Joseph wanted to administer the sacrament to the group. He went to get wine for the sacrament, but was stopped by a heavenly messenger. This messenger told Joseph that it did not matter what they ate or drank during the sacrament, but that if they were going to use wine, they should only use wine they had made themselves, and not any that their enemies may make for them.
  - **This revelation clarified that it does not matter what food or drink is used for the sacrament, and reiterates that our intent while taking the sacrament is the true purpose.**

- **About a month later, the Smiths were back in Fayette at the Whitmer home.** Their short refuge back in Harmony had been disrupted by persecution, and the Whitmers gladly took Joseph and Emma in again. It was here that Joseph learned about what Hiram Page had been up to. Hiram was married to Catherine Whitmer, David Whitmer's sister. Hiram had been one of the Eight Witnesses of the Book of Mormon the previous summer. Hiram had recently started using what he referred to as a seer stone in order to receive revelation for the entire Church. Many people were listening to and believing what Hiram Page was teaching, including Oliver Cowdery. When Joseph realized how wide-spread these beliefs were, he asked for and received the revelation known as D&C 28 for Oliver. **The Lord did 2 things in this Section: Oliver was called on a mission to the Native Americans, and the Lord clarified that only the prophet would receive revelation for the entire Church.**
  - **This revelation clarified one of the roles of the prophet,** confirming that only the prophet could receive revelation for the entire Church. However, the Lord made it abundantly clear, even in that very same revelation, that personal revelation and the ability to teach are available to all faithful members.

Spiritual Themes:

Look for these themes as you read this week! Find examples in the scriptures, and ponder on what these themes can look like in your life.

- **Purpose of the Sacrament**

- **Putting on the Armor of God**

- **Stewardship and Revelation**

People to Know:

- **Oliver Cowdery**
  - Oliver Cowdery started as a young school teacher who lived at the Smith family home in Manchester. He became friends with David Whitmer and the Whitmer family, and David and Oliver became interested in what Joseph Smith was doing.
  - Oliver joined Joseph in Harmony and became his scribe during the Book of Mormon translation process. Oliver and Joseph received the Aaronic priesthood together. Oliver helped Joseph and Emma find refuge with the Whitmer family when persecution grew in Harmony.
  - Oliver was one of the Three Witnesses of the Book of Mormon and the second elder of the Church during its organization.
  - Oliver received more revelations, along with Joseph, in July of 1830. In September of that year, he was asked to correct Hiram Page's false revelations, and officially called to serve a mission to the Native American tribes in Western Missouri.
- **Hiram Page**
  - He was married to Catherine Whitmer (David Whitmer's sister, and Peter and Mary's daughter). In June of 1829, he was able to be one of the Eight Witnesses to the Book of Mormon on the Smith farm in Manchester.
  - In September 1830, after the organization of the Church, Hiram had a stone where he was claiming to receive revelation for the entire Church. A concerned Joseph received a revelation asking Oliver to speak with Hiram and correct his errors of deception.

Where are We?

- **Harmony, Pennsylvania**
  - Emma Hale Smith's family lived in Harmony. Joseph and Emma lived here during much of the translation of the Book of Mormon, with Martin Harris and Oliver Cowdery assisting at various times. The Aaronic priesthood was restored in the nearby woods.
  - After persecution in Harmony started to grow, Joseph, Emma, and Oliver moved to Fayette to finish translating the Book of Mormon. They kept their home and farm in Harmony, returning from time to time throughout 1830 to tend to the farm, and take care of other business.
  - By July 1830 though, it was revealed that Joseph should focus all his time and efforts on building up the Church. The Lord gave Emma a special revelation in her time of uncertainty here in Harmony prior to their final departure.
- **Fayette, NY**
  - This is where the Whitmer family lived. Joseph, Emma, and Oliver moved here for a time to finish the Book of Mormon translation and organize the Church in April 1830.
  - This became the unofficial church headquarters for the remainder of 1830, with a church conference being held here in September. A few men received mission calls or other personal revelations during this conference. Many new prospective converts were sent to Fayette, and many were subsequently baptized or called on missions.

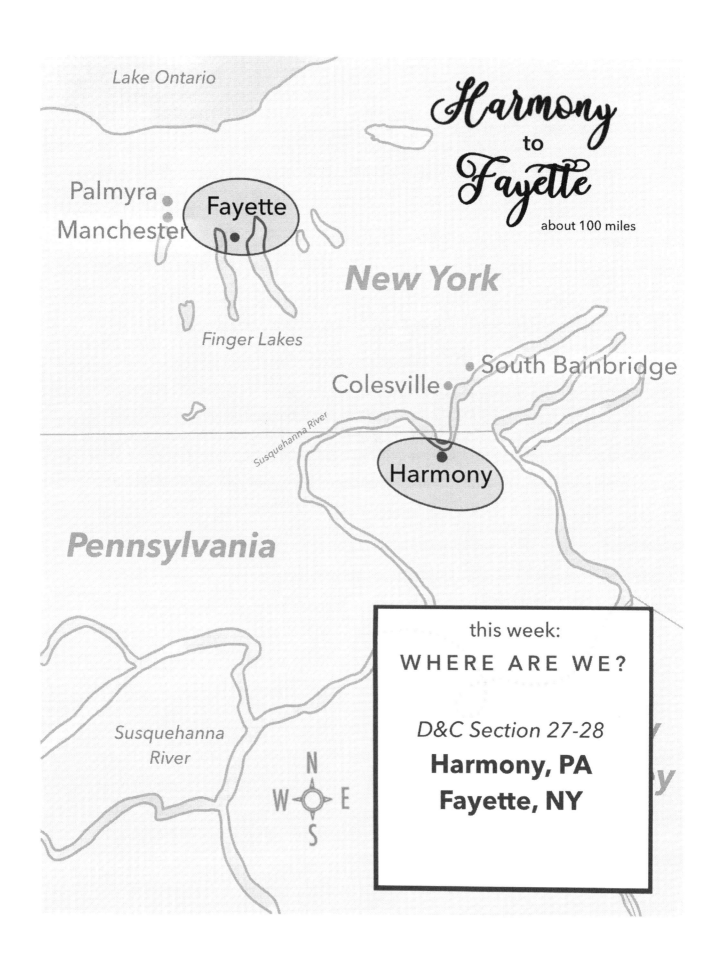

Lake Ontario

Harmony
to
Fayette
about 100 miles

Palmyra
Manchester

Fayette

New York

Finger Lakes

South Bainbridge

Colesville

Susquehanna River

Harmony

Pennsylvania

Susquehanna
River

N
W · E
S

this week:

WHERE ARE WE?

D&C Section 27-28
Harmony, PA
Fayette, NY

LITTLE PICTURE

How to understand each section and apply principles to my life

- **D&C 27:**
    - **Revelation Given Through:** Joseph Smith
    - **Revelation Given To:** The Church
    - **Revelation Given When/Where:** August 1830 in Harmony, Pennsylvania
    - **Before You Read:** This is a message Joseph received from a heavenly messenger as Joseph was trying to procure wine for the sacrament.
    - **What You'll Read About:** Joseph is told that it doesn't matter what you eat or drink for the sacrament, as long as it is done while focused on God. In a future day, we will partake of the sacrament with ancient prophets and other righteous people. We are instructed to put on the armor of God.

- **D&C 28:**
    - **Revelation Given Through:** Joseph Smith
    - **Revelation Given To:** Oliver Cowdery
    - **Revelation Given When/Where:** September 1830 in Fayette, New York
    - **Before You Read:** Hiram Page, one of the eight witnesses of the Book of Mormon, was claiming to receive revelations for the whole Church. Several members, including Oliver Cowdery, had been deceived.
    - **What You'll Read About:** The Lord teaches that only the prophet can receive revelations on behalf of the Church. Oliver is counseled to teach and speak by the Spirit, but not to command the whole Church because those keys are with Joseph. Oliver Cowdery is called on a mission to the native tribes west of Missouri, and should privately tell Hiram Page that his stone is not of God.

SPIRITUAL GUIDING QUESTIONS

Question: How do you remember the Savior during the sacrament? How does remembering Jesus make your sacrament participation more meaningful? (D&C 27:2)

Question: Which part of the armor of God are you best at "putting on"? Which is the hardest for you to "put on" right now? (D&C 27:15-18)

Question: What is something that our current prophet has recently taught? How have you shown your obedience to his teaching? (D&C 28:3)

Question: When is a time you received personal revelation for how to fulfill a calling or assignment at Church? What was that experience like? (D&C 28:4)

Question: Do you know who you have the authority to receive revelation for, either in your callings or in your family? Do you know who you do not have the authority to receive revelation for? (D&C 28:4-6)

Question: How do you think Oliver felt receiving this mission call? (D&C 28:8)

Question: How does Satan still deceive people today? How can you avoid being deceived? (D&C 28:11)

ADDITIONAL THOUGHTS AND NOTES

Congratulations for finishing Jan - March in the Doctrine and Covenants!

Ready for more scripture study resources?

Keep the momentum going!

Check comefollowmestudy.com or my social media channels @comefollowmestudy for more information on how to get your next Doctrine and Covenants Study Guide! Thank you for your continued support.

Got any questions or feedback? I'd love to hear from you at caliblack@comefollowmestudy.com.

Made in the USA
Las Vegas, NV
27 December 2024

15459234R00070